TRIBAL INDIA

Ancestors, Gods, and Spirits

TRIBAL INDIA

Ancestors, Gods, and Spirits

EDITED BY SARYU DOSHI

to
Roshan Sabavala
in grateful remembrance

Roshan Sabavala's untimely death on the 27th March 1992 is deeply mourned not only by the staff of MARG Publications, but by all her friends and admirers in the Tata Organisation. While many know about her keen personal involvement in MARG, few know that she was one of the Founder-Members of MARG in 1946, and since 1976 actively involved in the work of MARG Publications as General Adviser.

Some, if not all, of the readers and well-wishers of MARG books and journals will know how much MARG Publications owe to her steadfast dedication and her formidable determination that the published material should always be of international standards of excellence.

In this tribute to a very fine spirit who is much missed, the deepest sympathy of all who mourn the passing of Roshan Sabavala is extended to her devoted husband and children, Sharokh, Radhika and Tara Sabavala, who shared her love of MARG and worked hard in support of her aims and ideals.

(J. J. BHABHA)

Editorial Executives
SUDHA SESHADRI
L. K. MEHTA

Editorial Assistant
ARNAVAZ BHANSALI

Designer and
Production Manager
BEHROZE J. BILIMORIA

Design Assistant
SHANTANU ROY CHOUDHURY

General Manager—Finance
K. P. S. NAMBIAR

ISBN : 81-85026-18-1
Library of Congress Catalog Card
Number : 92-903563

RS. 1095

© MARG PUBLICATIONS, 1992.

This edition may be exported from
India only by the publishers, Marg
Publications, and by their authorized
distributors and this constitutes a
condition of its initial sale and its
subsequent sales.

Published by J. J. Bhabha for Marg
Publications at 24, Homi Mody Street,
Bombay 400 001.

Colour Processing by Comart
Lithographers Private Limited,
Bombay 400 025.

Printed by A.S. Vadiwala at
the Tata Press Limited,
Bombay 400 025, India.

CONTENTS

Roshan Sabavala, to whom this volume is dedicated, was a personal friend and we worked together, during my editorship at Marg to make it a publication of international repute. Her passion for excellence was my inspiration and her uncompromising approach my constant support.

Ever since its inception in 1946 Marg Publications has served as a pathway to the intricacies of Indian art and culture. In this quest, it has discussed the parallels and connections between the two great civilizations of India and Greece, presented the dynastic arts of the Guptas, and highlighted the contribution of a particular community such as the Muslim or the Jain. In some issues, it has adumbrated the character of a specific city like Calcutta or focused on the distinctive style and characteristics of eminent artists such as those at the Mughal court. In this volume Marg presents another facet of Indian art—the art of tribal India.

As is the case with many pioneering efforts, we encountered several problems while collecting material for this volume, the most frustrating of which was obtaining photographs of authentic tribal art from all parts of India. Although several anthropological treatises on various Indian tribes exist, their art has not been compiled. Only Verrier Elwin's lifelong work among the tribals of central and north-east India, fortunately, has preserved for us their traditions in the visual arts. But for other regions there is a distressing paucity of information on the tribal environment, their arts, and their legends. Most museums have not yet begun to collect the representative tribal art-forms in their regions nor has there been a systematic attempt at documentation in the Tribal Research Institutes that have been set up in various regions. It is for this reason that we could not present the tribal arts of the Himalayan and northern regions in this volume nor could we provide a detailed coverage of the extant tribal cultures of southern India.

Most tribal art activity, when not decorative, is ritualistic in intent. The art object loses its validity after the religious rites have been performed and is then discarded. Owing to this practice, tribal art objects are rare and thus not easily available. In recent years, however, the forcefulness of tribal art has caught the connoisseur's eye and many items are currently on sale in the art market. Not surprisingly some doubts have been raised as to whether such items are completely authentic, and in some cases there is even speculation as to whether the objects have been executed by the tribals themselves. But in the absence of adequate documentation, it is difficult to distinguish between the original and its simulations.

Some of the examples reproduced in this volume may be of recent origin, but have been included because their vision is true to the known tribal stylistic expressions. They appear to be examples of a continuing living tradition which functions within its prescribed framework in a changing tribal ethos. Some of these objects may be indistinguishable from art-forms of rural India, but this can be attributed to the cultural osmosis that has existed for generations between the tribal and the rural communities.

Today, the tribal communities are in the midst of an identity crisis as their way of life is disintegrating with the inroads of modern materialistic culture. Their art traditions are threatened because the beliefs and values that initiated them and sustained them are crumbling. Already much has vanished and much is being extinguished in the name of progress. Whatever art exists, shows dilutions in quality signalling lack of confidence: the conviction that pervaded it earlier is now ebbing away.

This volume is the first step in documenting some of the prevailing art-forms. It is hoped that the volume will inspire serious studies of the subject and encourage efforts towards recording tribal art-forms in remote areas which have not yet lost their pristine beauty.

Both, Marg Publications and myself are greatly indebted to Dr Laxmi Sihare, who as Director of the National Museum, New Delhi, suggested this theme to us in February 1991.

We are grateful to Dr R. C. Sharma, Director General, National Museum, for his kind permission to reproduce objects from the archives and collections of the museum.

The concept of the volume was developed under the learned guidance of Dr A. K. Das, Keeper, Anthropology, National Museum. His advice and assistance in the conception, planning, and compilation of this volume has been of inestimable value. We thank him profusely for his unstinted support in our endeavour. We are indebted to Smt Jayashri Sharma, Deputy Keeper, for her untiring efforts in assembling the illustrations from the photographic archives of the National Museum.

Shri K. K. Nayudu, I.A.S., Director, and Shri Uttamrao Sonawane, Curator of the Tribal Research and Training Institute, Pune, very kindly permitted us to reproduce the relevant objects from their collection of the tribal arts of Maharashtra. We are very grateful to them.

We extend our special thanks to the connoisseurs and collectors, Professor Sankho Choudhuri, Dr and Mrs Siddharth Bhansali, and Mr and Mrs Chester Herwitz for their generosity in permitting us to reproduce important and rare objects from their respective collections. The inclusion of these works of art has enhanced the understanding of the subject by imparting to it greater breadth and depth.

We express our grateful thanks to the Ministry of Human Resources, Department of Culture, Government of India for their encouragement and support in the compilation of this volume.

Marg Publications
is deeply indebted to

THE TATA OIL MILLS COMPANY LIMITED

for their encouragement and support
in producing this volume

A TRADITION IN TRANSFORMATION

SARYU DOSHI

In India the tribal population is revered as the *adivasis,* the original inhabitants of the land. The invading Aryans encountered them when they came thundering on their horses in the second millennium AD. These aborigines had lived in this land many centuries before the arrival of the Aryans, when an urban civilization flourished on the banks of the River Indus in the third millennium BC. Although the relationship between these people and the inhabitants of the cities of the Indus Valley Civilization is not quite clear, the presence of the tribals in that culture can be inferred from an impressive figurine of a dancing girl, representing an aborigine. Her skilfully rendered face reveals large eyes, flat nose, and bunched curly hair. Proud and confident in her bearing, the figurine is nude and wears several bangles on her arm. The modelling of the figure, especially her tubular limbs, corresponds to images currently being fashioned in rural and tribal India. Similarly, the terracotta animal figures from the Indus Valley Civilization exhibit many parallels to present-day tribal terracottas, their powerful rendition and enigmatic character denote a tradition that has remained essentially unchanged in technique and form over five millennia – from 3000 BC to AD 2000.

Over the centuries advances in agricultural techniques and military technology inevitably led to the phenomenon of simpler cultures becoming incorporated into the society of their powerful neighbours – the settled agriculturists. Gradually, due to acculturation, the peasant cultures absorbed and inducted most of the tribal communities except those that lived in the very distant and inaccessible parts of the land. There, beyond the pale of urbanization, in inhospitable corners of the land, in hilly tracts, and dense forests, the tribal communities remained self-contained and self-supporting in their self-imposed seclusion. They lived chiefly as hunters and food gatherers, practising *jhum* (shifting cultivation). The implements they used were simple and basic – a digging stick for tubers, a fire drill for ignition, spears as well as bows and arrows for attack and defence, traps for hunting, and various types of nets for fishing. Even today they live in the same manner and in many ways theirs is a world remote in time and space from ours.

The tribals in India live predominantly in the hills and plateaus that stretch in a curve from the east to the west separating the north from the south. Along this spine, in the fastness of the forests they have made their home. Apart from this region, tribal settlements exist in the Himalayan ranges in the north and north-east as also in the plains of Bihar and Bengal, and in some isolated pockets of southern India. Even when they live amid other communities they tend to remain aloof from the others. The tribals of the north-eastern region belong to Mongoloid stock, whereas those in the plains and peninsular India are mostly of proto-Australoid descent. A tribe in Gujarat – the Sidis – are descendants of Africans who came to India many centuries ago.

The tribal way of life has been generally described as primitive but it would be a mistake to assume that the appellation symbolizes an earlier strata in the evolution of the human culture. For, primitive societies do not represent a fossilized remnant of a bygone era, but have their own dynamics which provide energy and vigour to their culture. As Claude Levi Strauss, the eminent anthropologist stated: "They are not a backward or a retarded people, indeed they may possess in one realm or another a genius for invention or action that may leave the achievements of other people far behind."

Actually, the imaginative faculties and the emotional states of the tribals are rich and complex. They stem from a way of life which is circumscribed by religious beliefs and age-old

1

traditions. Their myths and customs derive their validity as well as their vitality from a past stored in the collective subconscious of the community. In this ethos rituals and festivals chart the cyclic course of the years, the coming and going of seasons, the waxing and waning of the moon, and rising and setting of the sun.

In the same way, rites and rituals punctuate the transitions in an individual's life as he or she traverses from one phase to another : birth, puberty, marriage, parenthood, and death. Beyond this world of self, family, and community lies the other world, a shadowy world of ancestors, spirits, and divinities – a world barely understood, but deeply felt and feared. The all-pervading invisible superhuman forces take the form of malevolent and benevolent spirits. The evil spirits need to be constantly propitiated by means of magico-religious rituals and sacrifices. The other spirits, though benevolent, are quick to take offence and need to be kept in good humour by proper offerings at appropriate times. Only then will their aid be forthcoming and their enemity avoided. A favourable equilibrium in life can be ensured by offering continuous worship. Connections to these mysterious powers can be established through a shaman and maintained by means of rituals prescribed for propitiation, supplication, and appeasement. In addition to serving a magico-religious purpose, the tribal rituals and ceremonies keep alive, from one generation to another, the myths and legends of the tribe, its religious beliefs and superstitions, its social ethics, and cultural identity.

The sacred image in tribal society can often be general and featureless – a beautifully rounded stone or an anthropomorphic image, complete with its specific attributes and animal vehicle. Both represent an instinctive expression of reality as perceived and apprehended by that particular tribal community. Integral to the worship of the divine principle are sculpted objects – in wood, metal, or clay or floor patterns executed in line or colour. Most tribal works of art are perishable: sculpture in wood or terracotta crumble while paintings are wiped out or fade away. Only metal objects survive the onslaught of time. Usually objects are created to last the duration of the ceremony or ritual and once it has served its purpose it loses its *raison d'être* and is discarded because it has become redundant. Like the performing arts, the visual arts in a tribal ethos are ephemeral. Most of the arts are used in conjunction: they do not exist as separate categories but as correlated activities. Often painting is executed to the accompaniment of a religious chant.

The aesthetic faculty appears to be innate in the tribal and perhaps first manifested itself in a desire to decorate his own person and the world around him. He adorns his body with paint which is temporary having no lasting effects or by scarification or tattoo which leave permanent marks on the body. The Jarawas and the Onges of the Nicobar Islands apply thick paint in broad curving strokes along the contours of the body. These designs are decorative in intent as are the tattoo patterns among certain tribes in Gujarat and Madhya Pradesh. But, in many tribes the tattoo impressions are associated with status. In the north-eastern region the tattoo marks on the chest of a man indicate his status as a head-hunter. Again, among some tribes in the north-east a certain form of tattoo is associated with a particular stage in the life of a woman. Particular designs at specific sites on the body – arms, legs, stomach – are associated with the onset of puberty, marriage, and the first pregnancy. On each occasion the woman is tattooed appropriately. Tattoo markings on the body in some tribes of the north-eastern region carry connotations of status; the more elaborate generally being equated with a position commanding greater privilege. In addition to body decoration, there is body adornment in the form of ornaments. The tribals exhibit an irrepressible urge to bedeck themselves with ornaments in the hair, around the head, in the ears, and the nose; on the body in the form of necklaces, necklets, armlets, bangles, waistbands, and anklets.

Since they have limited access to manufactured ornaments which have to be obtained from metalsmiths from nearby towns and villages, they fashion their own from materials that are easily available in their environment such as gum from trees, stalks, reeds, shells, artificially coloured hair, and feathers. These, they string in imaginative and innovative combinations often with cheap glass beads purchased from the village shopkeepers. From the humble commonplace materials they create amazingly artistic items. Some tribes prefer to cover themselves with ornaments, eschewing clothing. In certain tribes like the Bondos of Orissa the women wear numerous metal collars and beaded necklaces in subtly blended colours which completely conceal the upper part of their bodies. This profusion of ornaments is balanced by a bald shaven head, a brief skirt, and bare legs scantily adorned.

Even though some tribals wear limited clothing, they display immense ingenuity in the

2

manner in which they attire themselves in wool, silk, cotton, and even bamboo. The cloth, particularly in the north-east, is made by the tribal women themselves on small looms. They embellish the textiles with woven patterns in stylized configurations of inexhaustible variety inspired from nature – ripples on water, leaf clusters on a tree, or the peaks and valleys in a mountain range. The harmonious rhythm and hypnotic symmetry in nature are conveyed by geometric forms of triangles, hexagons, or zigzags. Curvilinear designs occur rarely, if at all.

The delicate designs on the wings of a butterfly and the repetitive pattern on the serpent also serve as a source of inspiration. A legend among the Sherdukpen tribe tells of a girl who falls in love with a handsome young man who, in reality, was a snake. Whenever she sat down to weave, he would assume his snake form and lie coiled in her lap. She copied the markings on her lover's body and as a result produced the most beautiful cloth ever seen.

In the southern regions as well, geometrical designs prevail. The Todas of Nilgiri embroider a shawl called the *putkuli* made of coarse cotton cloth purchased from the market. Two pieces of this cloth are sewn together, and the ends decorated with red and black stripes produced by the combined method of darning and embroidery. The embroidery is executed by counting of threads, resulting in angular forms. Against this sober palette of red and black, the Banjaras, known also as the Lambadis, use bright bold contrasting colours dramatized with pieces of glass and mirrors edged with embroidery, and cowrie shells edging the garments.

Among the Wanchos of the north-east the deft use of colour produces a raised effect in certain areas providing an additional dimension to the purely surface design. Here again, the forms are geometrical and their appeal lies in their directness and simplicity. Unfortunately, the tribals are now turning away from these traditional handspun and handwoven garments, depending increasingly on easily available synthetic and mill-made fabrics.

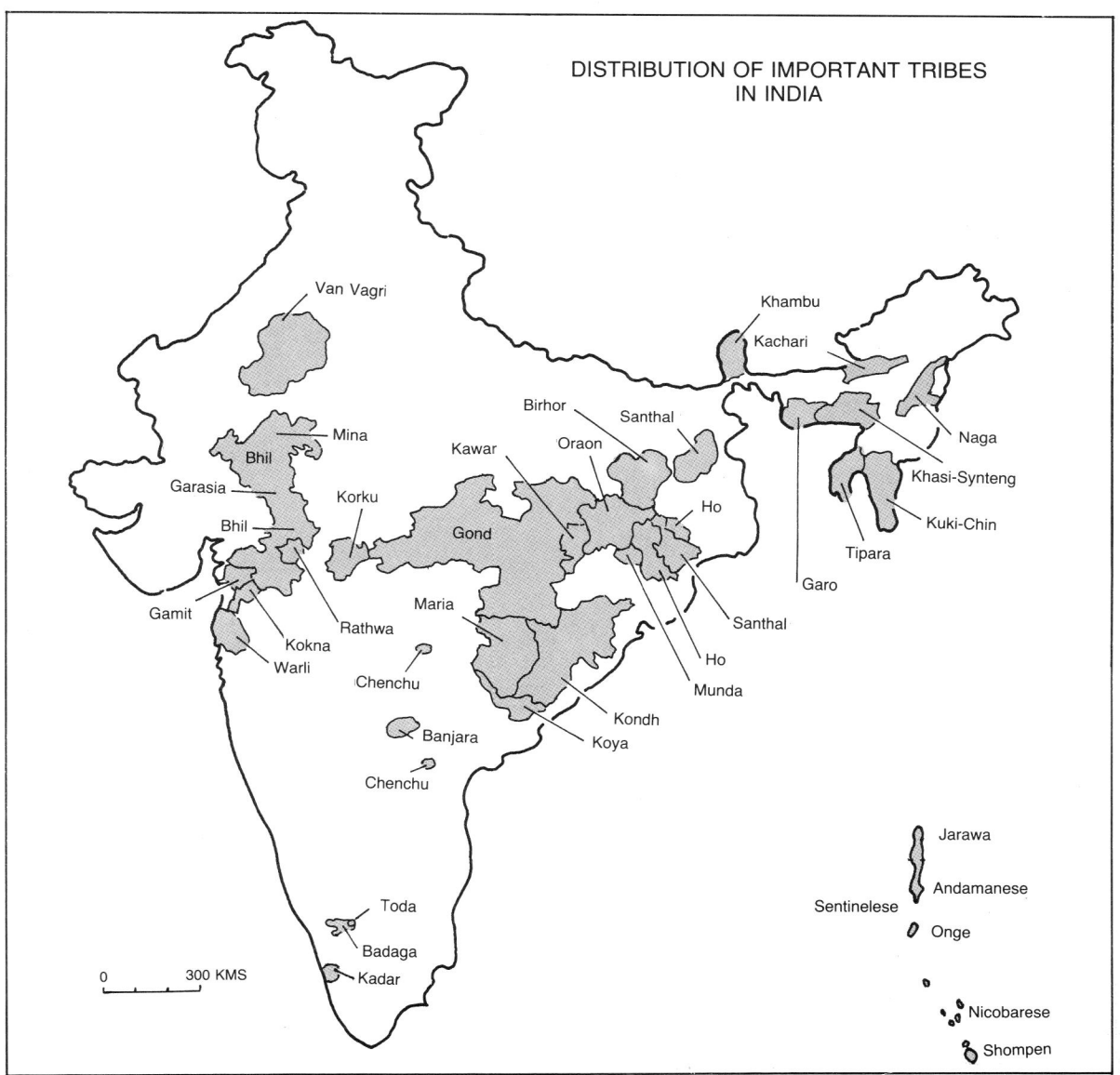

1. The distribution of important tribes in India shows a distinct pattern and is predominantly in the hilly regions.
Map courtesy Deccan College, Pune.

The tribal ensemble includes many traditional accessories such as tusks, feathers, tufts or coloured animal hair, grass stalks, wooden or bamboo hair combs, and metal hairpins. These are often imaginatively combined with inexpensive modern baubles like fluorescent ribbons, plastic flowers, metal filigree hair clips to produce a colourful and picturesque effect without detracting from its tribal character. More than other ornaments the hairpins and hair combs appear to have symbolic importance. The symbolism differs from tribe to tribe. In the north-east for example, the hairpin is worn by men and signifies success in a head-hunting expedition. In Maharashtra, the women wear the hair comb as a mere decorative ornament while in Bastar, in central India, it acquires romantic overtones as it is gifted by a man to his beloved. Among the Kaders of Kerala, it is customary for a young man to present his bride with a comb at the time of marriage, and this act is an essential feature of the ritual. Among the Muduvars, the comb serves as an indication of the married status of the woman.

The impulse to adorn extends from their person to their belongings – the digging stick, spear handles, hair combs and hairpins, pouches and containers for tobacco, household objects, musical instruments, and the house itself. The artistry is evident in the choice of the shapes as also in the proportions of the objects. In certain items such as baskets, the sensibilities project themselves in the exquisite workmanship and the manner in which certain techniques — pleating, twisting, and lattice work — have been combined with one another to produce the desired shape and effect. Objects of everyday use are decorated with etched designs which generally tend to be incipient in their expression and geometric in form consisting of lines, zigzags, triangles, and chevrons. The motifs are arranged in interesting configurations defining or being defined by the object on which they occur. Only an occasional example reveals ambitious effort as in the case of a musical instrument from south India which carries the depiction of a tiger chasing a stag or a Santhal fiddle shaped like a woman, which through its distortion and simplifications exhibits an inherent feeling for sculptured form.

The tribal home is decorated with designs that range from the simple to the highly intricate, from painted forms to patterns in low relief or a combination of both. In Orissa, the tribals enlivened their homes with broad bands of earth colours – yellow ochre, reddish brown, and white. In Madhya Pradesh the designs are executed in low relief and certain parts accentuated in colour. In the tribal homes in Gujarat, entire walls are covered with designs painted in white, charming in their regularity. The mud plastered wall is divided with wide vertical panels within which parallel horizontal bands carry geometrical designs interspersed with floral and vegetal motifs. The repetition of forms – sometimes treated as solids at other times as voids – provide a continuing rhythm and vitality to an otherwise static composition. Occasionally, in this conventional design a discordant note is struck by the introduction of a new and totally unrelated motif to the tribal milieu – of a tractor, a truck or a bus. Lately, with the opening up of the tribal areas as also the development programmes initiated by the Government of India for the upliftment of the tribal communities, these vehicles are encountered regularly in the remote regions. Fascinated by the advent of such vehicles into their hitherto isolated world, they incorporate them into their work. Not only trucks and buses, but also helicopters and aeroplanes feature in tribal art.

Auspicious wall-paintings among the Warli tribe of Maharashtra are executed with rice powder paste by women at the time of a marriage in the family. It depicts the goddess Palaghut in a sacred space, outside it are the bride and groom, and scenes of everyday life. In the last few years this tradition has moved out of the religious context and is no longer the forte of women. Men of the Warli tribe now practise this art-form. It has changed in content, though not in style and is produced for an entirely new patron – the urban art collector.

In Gujarat, several tribes believe in the god Pithora and paintings of the god, his consort, and his entourage together with a retinue of horses and elephants are featured on the hut walls. The depiction is enlivened by episodes from tribal mythology as also scenes of everyday life. Colourful and striking, these paintings are significant as votive offerings. Often, all the walls of the tribal hut are covered with paintings offered to the god Pithora. The painting of Pithora goes on for a few days and is accompanied by feasting and dancing. This is an excellent example of collective art in which the entire community participates, contributing in whatever form they can – in the performance of the ritual, in preparing for the feast or in the dances of celebration.

The belief in the magico-religious among the Saora tribals of Orissa motivates the execution

2. Body decorations for *Holi* festival celebrations.
The urge for artistic expression among the tribal people manifests itself in body decorations. The adornment can be of temporary or permanent nature. Some decorations are connected with festivals and during the *Holi* celebration young men and boys paint their faces and bodies.
Gujarat.
Photo: courtesy and copyright Jyoti Bhatt.

4

of a pictograph on the wall of the tribal dwelling whenever untoward happenings trouble the family. The pictograph consists of a house or a temple together with horses and elephants. Through invocations and chants the family invites and induces the deity whose wrath it has knowingly or unknowingly incurred to come and reside in the home. The moment it takes up residence in the painted structure, it is trapped there and constrained from causing further havoc. These pictographs are painted in white on the internal surface of the hut wall.

Thus, in tribal art, the decorative fuses with the symbolic, the auspicious, the ceremonial, the votive, and the magico-religious. In every category the associations overlap and interconnect in a holistic manner and cannot be unravelled. It is the totality of vision and experience that is significant.

Of all the rituals that are performed as rites of passage, the most important are those that take place after death. For then the person passes from the "living" to the stage of the "living dead". These rites connected with the cult of the "living dead", are related to funerary practices and trace their origin to ancient times as revealed by the tombs discovered in the Nilgiri Hills. Interestingly, these tombs have yielded terracotta animal figures of unmistakable tribal conception. In the north-east also, great attention is paid to the tomb and it is loaded with the belongings of the dead. Among the Wanchos and Phoms of the north-east, it is also customary to fashion wooden effigies of the dead. Made from a single piece of wood they are summarily executed with their appropriate tattoo markings. They are carefully dressed, and placed in front of the tomb. These figures with melancholic beauty serve as a place of habitation for the soul of the deceased. After the proper rites have been performed, however, the images cease to live and are discarded. In some villages in the north-east, the effigy is made of latticed bamboo work having a ghost-like effect.

It is customary among many tribes to erect memorials to the dead. They believe that the spirit of the deceased needs a resting-place and a memorial tablet made of stone or wood serves the purpose. A carved or painted symbol on the tablet is personified as the dead person through the performance of requisite rites. Often, in the minds of the family members the tablet becomes the person it represents and often a male member will offer the tablet a puff from his *bidi* (native cigarette). The tablet receives worship regularly and as the "living dead", is regarded as being more accessible to his descendants than the higher divinities. The family members expect it to intercede for them whenever they are in trouble and need help.

The tribals approach their divinities with prayers and offerings of terracotta figures of horses and elephants as thanksgiving for boons already received, or to appease the deities' wrath or as an inducement to secure blessings which serve as protection against adversity. Such votive offerings are made singing by an individual or collectively by the inhabitants of a village to avert calamities like crops wilting from drought or wild animals lifting cattle and domestic animals such as pigs and goats. A number of votive terracottas have wheels. Earlier, such terracottas were thought to be toys but Dr Malti Nagar's researches reveal that these are votive terracottas used during the performance of the ritual wherein the devotee thanks the divinity for granting wishes. Whenever a tribal wishes to seek a boon he approaches the deity and vows that if his wishes are fulfilled he will offer his thanks to the deity by performing a prescribed number of circumambulations with an offering – a terracotta figure. If the deity accedes to his request then during the performance of the ritual the tribal goes round and round the deity, pulling his terracotta offering on wheels tied to a string behind him.

More often than not, the sacred sanctuaries of the tribals are situated in remote areas, in some mystical place in the mountains, near a river or in a dense grove. The tribals carry their votive offerings with great care over difficult terrains to the sanctuary and after the rituals leave them there, unguarded and uncared for, to decay, disintegrate, and return to their source – the mother earth. Votive offerings in Gujarat also take the form of wooden crocodile gods, commissioned in gratitude for the birth of a male child or for alleviating calamities. Sometimes votive offerings are made in the form of paintings on the walls of the tribal homes such as that of Pithora in Gujarat.

Although there is no overt magico-religious basis to it, the custom of head-hunting among the tribes in the north-east has great cultural significance. It has served as an inspiration to art activities such as the sculpting of wooden human figures and wooden human heads as well as carvings in low relief on drinking mugs. In the *morung* (men's dormitories) are relief carvings on the beams and pillars as also free standing sculptures. The sculpting of the figures

3. Bastar woman at the bazaar.
Tattooed and adorned with numerous ornaments the women of Bastar in Madhya Pradesh show juxtaposition of natural and manmade jewellery. The baskets, woven from bamboo and leaf serve as receptacles for storage. Madhya Pradesh.
Photo: courtesy collection of the late Sumant Moolgaokar — Padma Bhushan.

4. Scare-devil.
The hardships of living in the Nicobar Islands have made the inhabitants believe that their troubles are caused by malevolent spirits. The Nicobarese place their magico-mythical objects carved of wood inside or outside their homes to scare the devils away and protect the inhabitants of the home. Nicobar Islands.
Photo: courtesy and copyright Jyoti Bhatt.

5. The sacred mountain.
Among the Warlis of Maharashtra at the time of a marriage, the women of the family draw on the wall of the inner cell of the hut an auspicious painting of the Devi Palaghut. The painting is executed with rice paste on a reddish mud plastered wall.

In the last decade or so, the Warli men have taken up this art-form and freed it from its ritual constraints by employing it to depict everyday scenes and occurrences in their life. The results have a lively charm. Among these new expressions are encountered examples of X-ray art – a form common to many primitive societies in the world. These are the first known examples of this genre in India. Here the mountain is shown, as also the cave with the tiger, known to be there but not apparent to the eye.
Maharashtra.
Photo: Chandu Mhatre.

tends to be simplistic with little attempt at plasticity. The proportions of the figure are determined by the importance placed on the head as the most important part of the body. The treatment is summary, reducing the rendering of the facial features to strong and stark primary shapes of triangles and ovals.

Forms of tribal visual art such as masks and costumes accentuate the activities in the tribal rituals and dance-dramas that often follow the completion of a ritual. Certain masks – of animals and birds – tend to be naturalistic in order to be convincing, while others like those from Bengal possess an effete charm, and those from central India are expressionistic in style. In central India, as also the north-east there exists a tradition which portrays the diseased and the deformed. In many of the masks, the human facial features are transformed and abstracted into abbreviated forms – slits for the eyes and holes for the mouth. This simplification into basic shapes enhances its magical qualities and lifts it above the mundane. When the performing arts and the visual arts merge the experience of the numinous is heightened.

In the last two hundred years, if not more, the tribal communities have had close interactions with the peasant population of rural India. It is the village potter – often a woman – who makes the terracottas for the tribals according to their specific requirements. Similarly, the village silversmith fashions ornaments worn by the tribal women. Over a period of time this relationship between the forest tribals and the village peasants has caused influences to flow from one milieu to the other and contributed to a style that is tribal in spirit, but not in content. This style is evident in a number of diminutive but lively figures that appear to be produced

6. Goddess holding trident and bowl.
Over the centuries an ongoing process of osmosis between the tribals and their neighbouring village communities has led to deceptively similar art expressions. It is impossible to determine whether such images belong to the folk or the tribal milieu.
Coll: Dr Siddharth and Yashodhara-raje Bhansali.
Photo: Dr Siddharth Bhansali.

7. Mother with children.
In the self-contained world of the tribals the art-forms were imbued with power and strength. The exposure to the outside world has begun to dilute its quality as in this figure, where forcefulness has yielded to mellifluousness in style.
Coll: National Museum, New Delhi.
Photo: courtesy National Museum, New Delhi.

6

7

9

8. Decoration of a house.
The exposure to the outside
world has had its impact on tribal
art. In many places new motifs
intrude into traditional designs
and it is not unusual to observe a
truck incorporated into a panel
featuring geometrical and
stylized motifs. Though
somewhat disconcerting the
effect is very interesting. Other
innovations in tribal art occur in
combining forms that hitherto
belonged to separate traditions
as in this home. Here, the
traditional *jali* decoration is
reinforced by the presence of a
votive terracotta animal and a
human figure which though
tribal in its inspiration belongs to
an unidentifiable tradition. The
juxtaposition of forms is
harmonious. Such innovative
interpretations of existing
traditions will lead tribal art to
develop in new directions.
Madhya Pradesh.
Photo: courtesy and copyright
Jyoti Bhatt.

9. Rathwa women.
Bejewelled abundantly, the
women attend *Holi* fairs,
where the tribals buy and sell
goods.
Gujarat.
Photo: courtesy and copyright
Jyoti Bhatt.

9

near the pilgrimage city of Nasik in Maharashtra. The figures represent Hindu divinities but their rendering certainly harks back to some tribal deity that served as a model. These figures have large disproportionate heads, pointed faces with huge eyes, and flat planar bodies with rudimentary modelling and spindly limbs. In the same style and from the same centre are some remarkable representations of Shaivite shrines. Their composition recalls some archaic shrine under a tree rather than a Hindu temple where Shiva is generally worshipped.

The animal terracottas as well as the Hindu metal images from Nasik reveal that often tribal and village arts impinge on each other and occasionally the expression of both becomes blurred seeming to belong to both traditions and yet to neither. But apart from this area, on each side – tribal as well as village – are forms that are uncontaminated, assured, and assertive. Together they represent the pristine essence of art – tribal on the one side and folk on the other.

Who are the creators of tribal art? In fact, there is seldom a special class of artisans who undertake the work of carving or painting. Every member of the tribe sculpts or paints. In many tribal communities, it is the women who paint on the walls of the house and have learnt the art unconsciously and intuitively by watching other women decorating the walls of their homes. For the tribals, the arts are in their being, for not only can they sculpt or paint, but they can also sing and dance. Their arts embody their exuberance and serve to underline the cultural complexities that are capable of producing imagery of extraordinary aesthetic power. For, whether the tribal work of art is produced in the service of a magico-religious ritual or for pure decoration, the art is sincere and spontaneous, the articulation instinctive, its expressionistic vitality overriding elements of beauty.

The forms of tribal art may appear unchanging, but it is from their repeated renderings that the true form emerges – taut, tense, uncluttered, and assured. The iconography may be imbued with certitude but it leaves enough room for the creator to infuse it with his or her perceptions, prejudices, hopes, and aspirations. All over the world the abstract and expressionistic qualities of primitive art have displayed an inventiveness and originality that have seldom been equalled. Their aesthetic sense has evoked praise and admiration from eminent and celebrated early twentieth-century artists such as Picasso and Matisse. And though, at first, tribal art may strike one as disturbing, even disgusting, with greater familiarity the observer will be able to discern its compelling qualities and challenging aesthetic.

In India, in the past few decades, the tribal arts have steadily lost their vigour and vitality. Perhaps, it is inevitable, because at this time their culture is disintegrating with the constant inroads of modernization and development programmes for their upliftment. The tribals' confidence in their own ethos has been undermined, for they have been exposed to what they believe is a higher culture with its material wealth and superior technology. The situation is exacerbated by rapid means of transport which expose them to a wider world, by health schemes that have shown them the hollowness of rituals carried out to exorcise the demon causing sickness, and by education which makes them question the old and established values. A world that was once contained and coherent, has now splintered into fragments; they are confused and plagued with a sense of inferiority. It is only when the tribals have adjusted to new ways can their intuitive forces regroup and revive, perhaps, only then will they be able to mould their earlier way of life to fit the new setting, giving it meaning, and renewed form.

In the field of art this has already occurred in Maharashtra. The appreciation and accolade that greeted the Warli art motivated the men of the community to try their hand at a form that has been strictly a woman's domain. Not inhibited by tradition Jivya Soma started painting on paper and produced the most charming scenes of the Warli world – tribals dancing in a spiral, paddy fields with frogs, a spider's web strung between two trees or a tribal ritual in a cave shrine. He released the art from its religious and symbolic fetters and brought it into the realm of everyday experience. In doing so, he has taken recourse to the X-ray technique whereby he painted not only what he saw – the external form – but also what he could not see yet knew to be there: a mountain cave with a tiger seated within. Artists in various parts of the world have used this art-form but it has occurred in India for the first time and that too in a sphere that is not traditional. Hopefully the changing situation will direct trained skills to find a new aesthetic in keeping with their inherited traditions and vision.

TRIBAL SOCIETIES OF INDIA

MALTI NAGAR

About sixty million people of India (roughly seven per cent of the population) belong to what are variously known as tribes, scheduled tribes, aborigines, and *adivasis*. A number of other communities categorized as criminal tribes during the British period and now known as denotified tribes also belong to the same category. More than three hundred, including sub-groups, communities have been recognized as scheduled tribes by the central Government. Anthropologists do not agree upon a single definition of the term "tribe". But one can say that a tribe is a non-industrialized society which occupies a homogeneous territory, speaks a common language, and believes in a common ancestry.

Very often in anthropological literature the word "primitive" is used as a synonym for "tribe". However, the tribal communities are primitive only in respect of technology, economy, and material culture. Unless contaminated by contact with the so-called "civilized people", the tribal people cherish their own values of life. A pristine tribal society is characterized by the virtues of honesty, truthfulness, dignity of labour, egalitarianism, social cohesiveness, discipline, concern for fellow members of the society, equal status of women, and hospitality towards strangers. Evils such as dowry, prostitution, economic and social exploitation are unknown in tribal societies.

The puritanical attitude towards sex, so characteristic of Indian "civilized society", is alien to tribal culture. Young men and women are allowed to mix freely. In several tribal societies such as the Muria Gonds of Bastar (Madhya Pradesh) and the Oraons of Chota Nagpur (Bihar) there are youth dormitories in which the young of one or both sexes live and learn the values of their society. Tribal women are free to choose their life partners, and there is no stigma attached to divorce, widowhood, or remarriage.

Crass materialism or acquisitiveness which is such a distinctive feature of "civilized society" is unknown among the tribal peoples. Instead, the emphasis is on sharing of wealth and happiness. Disputes regarding property and women are settled amicably and the decision is binding on the disputing parties. Music, song, and dance are an integral part of tribal life. Even though both men and women dress scantily, they are fond of ornaments and decoration of the body. They put flowers in their hair and wear ornaments made of grass stalks, glass and plastic beads woven into necklaces, metal neckbands, bangles, and anklets. Although tribal languages had traditionally no written literature, they have a rich oral tradition of folk songs and folk tales. In their original habitat the tribal people live a healthy, happy, and carefree life.

Distribution

The tribal societies are mainly concentrated in the hilly and forested belt of the central part of the country extending from the Aravallis of Rajasthan through the Sahyadris of Gujarat and Maharashtra, the Vindhyas and Satpuras of Gujarat and Maharashtra, the Vindhyas of Madhya Pradesh and Uttar Pradesh, the Chota Nagpur plateau of Bihar and West Bengal, and the Eastern Ghats of Andhra Pradesh and Orissa to the many hill ranges of north-east India. Small tribal pockets are also found in the Nilgiris in Tamil Nadu and in the Western Ghats in Kerala. Scattered tribal people are found in all parts of the country including the intensively cultivated and densely populated Indo-Gangetic Plain. But here, living in the midst of more advanced peoples, they have lost their tribal identity and independence. Some of the tribals who behaved as caste groups are engulfed in the lower strata of society.

The numerically major tribes of India are: Bhils (Rajasthan, Gujarat, Maharashtra, and Madhya Pradesh); Gonds (Madhya Pradesh, Maharashtra, Andhra Pradesh, and southern part of Uttar Pradesh); Mundas, Santhals, and Hos (eastern Madhya Pradesh, Bihar, and West Bengal); Khasis, Jaintias, and Garos (Meghalaya); Bodos and Kacharis (Assam); Nagas (Nagaland and Manipur); and Mizos (Mizoram). Other tribes, prominent in anthropological literature, because of their distinctive economic and cultural traits are: Rathwas and Gamits in Gujarat; Kokna and Warli in Maharashtra; Korku and Kawar in Madhya Pradesh; Chenchus in Andhra Pradesh; Todas and Badagas in Tamil Nadu; Kadars, Paniyans, and Malapantarams in Kerala; Kondhs, Saoras, Gadabas, and Bondos in Orissa; Birhors in Chota Nagpur; Monpas, Adis, Nishis, and Mishmis of Arunachal Pradesh; Tiparas in Tripura and Kuki-Chin in Mizoram.

There is a general belief among social scientists that the tribal people have been pushed into their present marginal habitats from the fertile plains by the economically more advanced and aggressive farmers and townspeople. This belief has no basis to sustain it. The tribal people are concentrated in the hilly and forested central belt of the country because they have lived there for countless generations and that habitat is ideal for the kind of life they live. Plentiful archaeological evidence shows that the hills and forests of the central part of our country have been inhabited by human groups for several hundred thousand years. These prehistoric peoples lived entirely by hunting and gathering, and the present-day tribals are their descendants. Even though today many tribal communities practise some kind of primitive agriculture, all of them also practise a certain degree of hunting, fishing, and collection of wild vegetable food, medicinal and other economic products. These resources are available in greater abundance in the hills and forests than in the alluvial plains. Due to these ecological factors, hunting-gathering tribes are concentrated in the hilly and forested tracts.

In the pre-agricultural times, hunting-gathering tribes were spread all over the country. However, once agriculture began to be introduced in different parts of the country about five thousand years ago, primeval forests had to be cleared to make way for farms and settlements. The habitat of the hunter-gatherers was slowly destroyed. These people had no choice but to integrate themselves into the rural and urban economy.

Biological and Cultural Diversity

The numerous tribal societies of India are not a homogeneous biological, linguistic, or cultural entity. Instead, they are characterized by considerable diversity. Biologically, most of the tribes of peninsular India can be classified as belonging to the proto-Australoid stock. They are short of build, have a low forehead, flattish nose, dark complexion, and curly hair. On the other hand, the tribes of north-east India and of the Himalayas in Himachal Pradesh and Uttar Pradesh belong to the Mongoloid stock.

Linguistically, all the tribes of south India as well as the Gonds and Oraons of central India speak languages of the Dravidian family. The presence of Brahui in Baluchistan and of Kurukh in the Nepal Terai — both Dravidian languages — suggests that in the remote past, languages of this family were spoken over most of the subcontinent. The Khasis and Jaintias of Meghalaya, and the Mundas, Santhals, Kols, Hos, Saoras, Bondos, and Korkus of central India speak languages belonging to the Austro-Asiatic (or Mundari or Kolarian) family. Indeed, the presence of the Korku in the Hoshangabad area of Madhya Pradesh and of the Kol in the Gangetic Plain around Allahabad shows that these languages which are related to the Mon-Khmer languages of South-East Asia had penetrated deep into the heart of India. The close overlap between the distribution patterns of these languages and of certain types of neolithic stone celts, megalithic practices of disposal of the dead, and associated rituals has been interpreted by anthropologists to mean that these languages were introduced into India by people from South-East Asia who also brought with them early agriculture and megalithic ritual. Other tribes of north-east India and the Himalayas speak languages belonging to the Tibeto-Burman family. The tribes of Gujarat, Rajasthan, and the Indo-Gangetic Plain speak the local languages of the Indo-Aryan family although their languages also have words and grammatical structures which are alien to Indo-Aryan languages. It is believed that tribes such as the Bhils initially had their own distinctive languages but have lost them due to long contact with the economically and socially dominant Indo-Aryan speakers.

Economically too, there is a great diversity in the tribal population. There are small groups — the Van Vagris in western Rajasthan, the Birhors in Chota Nagpur, the Kanjars, the Baheliyas, and several others in the Gangetic Plain, the Kuchbandhias and the Pardhis in

1. Hill-Miri man.
Hailing from Arunachal Pradesh, he has Mongoloid features found in north-east India.
Arunachal Pradesh.
Photo : courtesy collection of the late Sumant Moolgaokar — Padma Bhushan.

14

2. Environment.
Art among the tribals is an inherent part of their everyday life.
Rajasthan.
Photo: courtesy and copyright Jyoti Bhatt.

3, 4. Tattoo designs.
Tattoo, a very common form of
decoration among tribal
communities, occurs on the
face, chest, arms, and legs
among both men and women.
More often than not its function
is decorative but as in some
tribes in the north-east, it can be
also symbolic.
Madhya Pradesh.
Fig. 3 : Photo courtesy and
copyright Jyoti Bhatt.
Fig. 4 : Photo courtesy Michel
Sabatier.

3

4

central India, the Chenchus and the Yenadis in the Eastern Ghats in Andhra Pradesh, and the Kadars, Paniyans, and Malapantarams in the Western Ghats in Kerala who live even today by hunting-gathering and, in some cases, fishing. Others like the Gujjars in the Western Himalayas, the Rabaris in Rajasthan and Gujarat, the Dhangars in Maharashtra and Karnataka, and the Todas of the Nilgiri Hills in Tamil Nadu live by pastoralism. In eastern and central India many tribes such as the Baigas in Madhya Pradesh, the Saoras, the Gadabas, the Parojas, and the Bondos in Orissa, the Garos in Meghalaya, and many tribes in the north-east live by shifting cultivation variously known as *dahiya, podu chasa,* or *jhum.* Most other tribes practise some kind of primitive plough agriculture, combining it with a certain amount of livestock rearing. Almost all of the other groups practise a certain degree of hunting-gathering and fishing depending upon the resources available in their environment. For the tribes of the Mongoloid stock and those speaking Kolarian languages, the cow is only an animal for meat as they are unfamiliar with the consumption of milk.

Historical Development

Until after the European missionaries began committing tribal languages to writing in the nineteenth century, tribal societies did not have literacy and therefore no recorded history. Hence it is not possible to correctly trace the antiquity of different tribes. However, archaeological evidence, as stated above, clearly shows that most of the areas inhabited by tribal peoples were colonized by stone age hunter-gatherers many thousands of years ago. And most of the tribal societies are probably direct descendants of these prehistoric peoples. From the time Indian history began to be recorded in datable oral and written literature, references to certain tribes appear. This suggests that at least for the last three-and-half thousand years tribal peoples have been a part of this country. Linguists tell us that Austro-Asiatic or Kolarian and Dravidian words occur in the Vedic and later Sanskrit literature. In the *Mahabharata* there is the story of Eklavya who is believed to have been a Bhil. In the *Ramayana* there is the story of Sabari who is believed to have been a woman of the Saora tribe living in the area identified

5. A tribal boy getting ready for the *Holi* festival.
The tribals of Gujarat celebrate the *Holi* festival for days together with abandon. On this occasion, young men and boys decorate their bodies with oranaments.
Gujarat.
Photo: courtesy and copyright Jyoti Bhatt.

5

6. Adornments.
Contact with the outside world has introduced metal hair clips, brightly coloured ribbons, paper flowers, and plastic baubles to the tribals. The tribal women from Bastar, exhibit immense ingenuity in the manner in which they combine these items with their traditional hair ornaments such as grass stalks, flowers, *bidis,* and feathers.
Madhya Pradesh.
Photo: courtesy and copyright Jyoti Bhatt.

6

as Dandakaranya. There are also references to the Nishadas and other tribes in this epic. In the later classical literature there are frequent references to forest dwelling hunter-gatherers. Both archaeological evidence and historical sources show that tribal people are indigenous to this country.

Acculturation

The culture of almost all the tribal peoples has been influenced by that of their Hindu neighbours depending on the length and degree of contact between the two. In the Indo-Gangetic Plain and other regions which have a long history of agriculture and settled rural and urban life, some of the tribals have been assimilated into society and relegated to a low status in the caste hierarchy. A number of tribes converted to Christianity.

In the interior hilly and forested areas where the contact between the tribals and non-tribals is of a shorter duration and less intense, the tribals managed to preserve their original culture in varying degrees. Here the process of contact was intensified after the establishment of the British rule when systematic forestry operations began and non-tribals – contractors, traders, and labourers – reached the tribal habitats. With the continuing growth in population in recent decades and the increasing demand for arable land, non-tribal farmers and traders have encroached upon tribal habitats on a massive scale. After Independence, exploitation of mineral resources such as coal and iron, which happen to be located in tribal habitats, and the establishment of industries have further accelerated this process.

This contact has wreaked havoc upon tribal society and culture. The venal contractors, traders, and rich farmers fully exploited the innocent tribals' weakness for liquor by giving them easy loans at exorbitant rates of interest. Unaccustomed to a money economy, the tribals were rapidly deprived of their land and reduced to penury. Poverty-stricken, their women fell easy prey to the lust of rapacious contractors, traders, landlords, and petty bureaucrats. Today most tribal people are an impoverished, famished, despondent lot, and present a pathetic sight. The music, song, and dance which were once an integral part of tribal life have gone out forever.

Art

In tribal society artistic activity is not a separate domain; it is inextricably linked to the mundane activities of everyday life and to the production of utilitarian objects. The tribal man and woman have a highly developed sense of beauty. Tribal settlements are remarkably clean and their houses elaborately and artistically made. The Bondos of Orissa, and the Khasis, Garos, Nagas, Mizos, and other tribes of north-east India weave beautiful textiles of bright colours. In fact, weaving is an essential qualification for every girl. The Toda men and women too, weave colourful textiles. All tribals make a variety of ornaments from vegetal materials available in their environment. Their musical instruments, hunting, agricultural, and fishing gear, dancing items, objects of household use, weapons of warfare such as spears, bows and arrows are all made, not only to serve their function efficiently, but also to look attractive. Most tribals are experts at making beautiful baskets from bamboo, cane, and other plant materials, as also articles of rope and wood. The Muria and Maria Gonds of Bastar, as also the Korkus of central India make interesting carvings on wooden memorial pillars. The metal work, specially sculpture, of the Gonds of Bastar is enticing though unsophisticated by modern standards.

Some of the tribal groups, the Rathwas of Gujarat, the Warlis of the Thane district of Maharashtra, the Gonds of central India, and the Saoras of Orissa decorate the walls of their houses and clay storage bins with beautiful paintings and appliqué designs of animals, humans, and other subjects. The motifs are highly stylized and have close parallels with the cave art of the Mesolithic hunter-gatherers and their descendants and appears to be its continuation. Tribal women and, to some extent, men are very fond of decorating their bodies with tattoo designs.

However, with the fast disintegration of tribal society and culture, their art too is disappearing. Fortunately, whatever is left of it, is being sustained by tourist demand and the newly awakened interest in ethnic things among the urban élite.

A.K. DAS

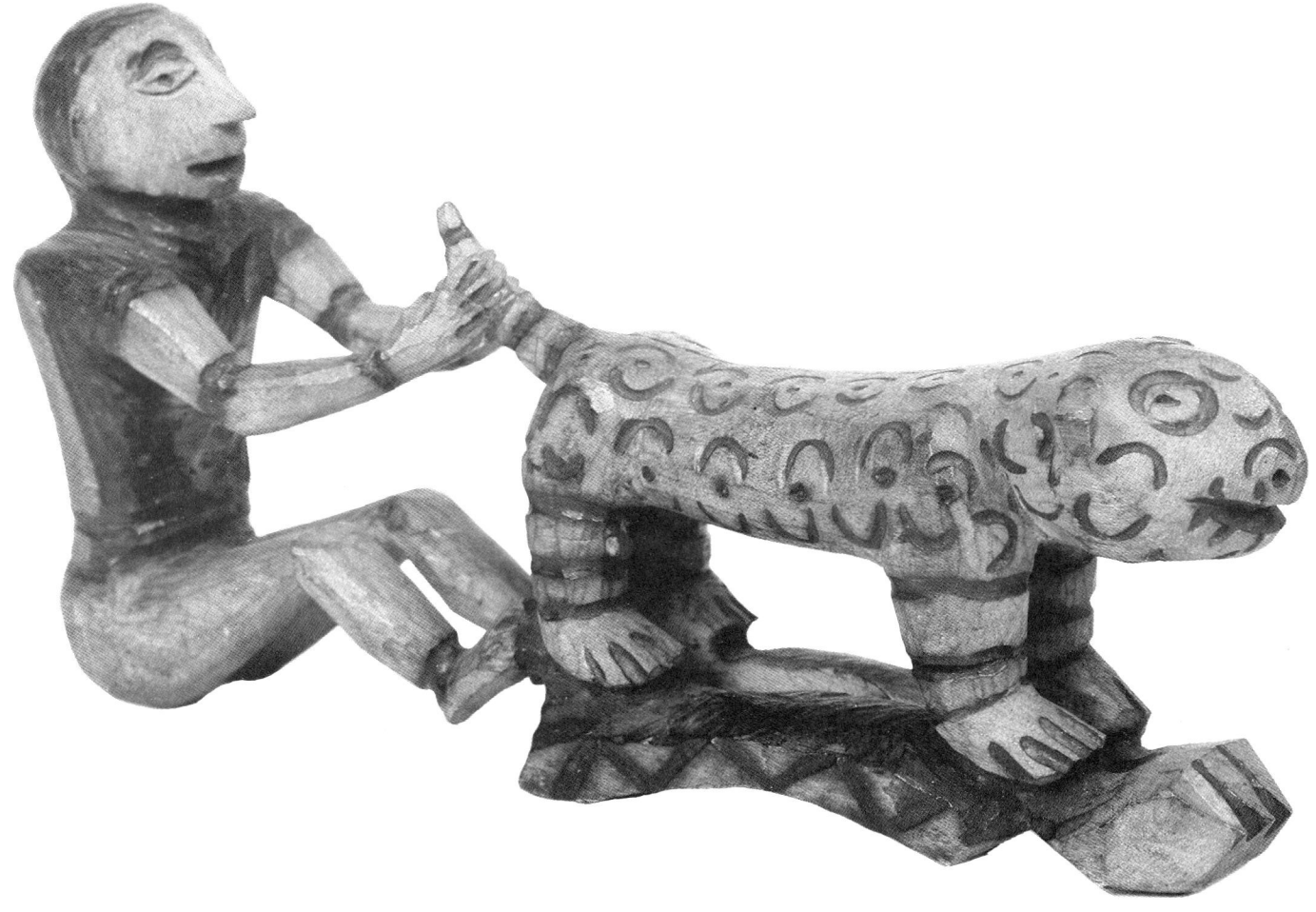

NORTH-EAST INDIA

The north-eastern corner of India is a mountainous and hilly enclave bounded on the north by the formidable Himalayan ranges and on other sides by South Asian countries such as Bhutan, Tibet, Myanmar, and Bangladesh with a narrow passage in the west for communication with the Gangetic Plain. This region comprises seven small states namely Assam, Arunachal Pradesh, Manipur, Nagaland, Meghalaya, Mizoram, and Tripura. The mighty Brahmaputra river flows majestically through this land and its tributaries have etched a permanent landscape of impenetrable jungle, marshy lands, and dense undergrowth. Here and there, patches of paddy fields terraced in the hillside indicate hamlets and villages. The topography and ecological diversity have shielded this region from the wider socio-cultural processes of the country.

The most significant feature of this region is its predominant tribal population. There are approximately seventy-five distinct tribes including sub-tribes in this area. Some of the major tribes from Arunachal Pradesh are the Monpas, Sherdukpans, Nishis, Apatanis, Adis, Mishmis, Wanchos, and Noctes. The Ao, Angami, Lotha, Sema, and the Konyak hail from Nagaland while the Tangkhul Kabui and the Kuki belong to Manipur. The Bodos, Rabhas, Karbis, Mishing, and the Kacharis live in Assam. The Khasis and Garos are natives of Meghalaya while the Riangs and the Jamatia inhabit Tripura.

Certain tribes in this region such as the Monpa, Sherdukpan, Khamti, and Singpho are adherents of the Buddhist faith. Numerous tribes in Nagaland, Mizoram, and Meghalaya have been converted to Christianity during the British rule. The Noctes of Tirap district in Arunachal Pradesh profess some sort of Vaishnavism unlike the remaining tribes who practise religions which centre around magico-religious beliefs and rituals. The cult of head-hunting was once prevalent among the Wanchos, the Noctes, and the Nagas.

The tribal arts of this region exhibit three distinct styles: one which is greatly influenced by the sophisticated Pan-Himalayan Buddhist art and the other two which are more indigenous in their inspirations. The influence of Buddhist Pan-Himalayan style is visible in the architecture of the great monasteries of Tawang, Diveng, and Kalaktang in Arunachal Pradesh as also in artefacts such as the Buddhist *thankas* (scroll paintings) and clay figurines of the Buddha. The native art styles are not as widely known, but are equally if not more interesting, because the artistic impulse is uninhibited and free from other stylistic overtones. It expresses itself in wood sculpture including masks, textiles, as well as in traditional ornaments, and apparel.

Wooden Images: Art of Power

The art of wood carving exists only in a few pockets in the north-eastern region. Among these, the most important is found in Arunachal Pradesh and Nagaland. The tradition of wood carving in these areas was once intimately connected with the cult of head-hunting, mortuary rites, decoration of the *morung* (bachelor's dormitory), and feasts of merit. The social and religious context has exercised considerable influence on the content as well as the style of the wooden objects.

Carved images belonging to the cult of head-hunting stand apart from the rest because of their iconography. They are found usually in a standing posture with one hand holding a *dao* (bill-hook) generally raised, as if in readiness to attack the enemy. Some of the figures hold a gun or spear instead of the *dao*. Occasionally, a rectangular shield is added and is held in the left hand. In some images the head-hunter is depicted with his victim who is of diminutive stature. The head-hunter holding the head of the hunted in one hand is a common theme. Generally, these wooden effigies are portrayed without any apparel, though occasionally a loin cloth or waistband is shown. A large number of head-hunter figures are ithyphallic which is not surprising as an erect phallus is construed to be a symbol of the warrior's potency and power. An exceptionally interesting cult effigy is a coiled-snake motif on the chest: this motif appears to represent the traditional sign of fertility.

In addition to the standing figures, the cult of head-hunting employed the motif of the carved wooden head. These were used as pendants or decorations on a dancer's basket. These ornaments occupy a definite place in the repertoire of Naga cult objects. Keeping in view its socio-religious value, the craftsman sculpts it with great care, makes special efforts to impart to it a realistic appearance. Some of the heads are carved in low relief, while others are three dimensional though sculpted in a very simplistic manner. Sometimes dyed hair is stuck on the head, and cowrie-shells, coloured beads or stones serve as eyes. The hair-style is indicated by black paint covering the top of the head, and sometimes the demarcation is indicated by a lightly incised line. The black colour gives the impression of hair on the head. The lips are

1. Man and tiger.
Stemming from the tradition of *morung* decoration this masterpiece has captured movement with a touch of humour. The decorations on the animal are achieved through the technique of burning and scorching the wood. The same technique with a slight variation is employed for the human figure as well.
Coll: National Museum, New Delhi.
Photo : courtesy National Museum, New Delhi.

2. A Naga warrior.
Body adornments in the form of tattoo marks and ornaments among the tribes of north-east India carry connotations of status.
Photo : courtesy collection of the late Sumant Moolgaokar – Padma Bhushan.

24

3. Apatani woman.
This woman with a tattooed
face wears traditional dress and
ornaments made from natural
materials such as seeds, bark,
and areca spathe. Blackened
cylindrical pieces used as nose
plugs are conventional
ornaments in this tribe.
Photo : courtesy collection of
the late Sumant Moolgaokar –
Padma Bhushan.

Wooden figures.
Wood carvings in the north-eastern region, particularly in Arunachal Pradesh and Nagaland are connected with the decorations of the morung (men's dormitory), head-hunting cult, and mortuary rites. The treatment is almost always simplistic.

4. Standing couple.
Secular in intent these figures are of extraordinary rendition.
Coll: National Museum, New Delhi.
Photo : courtesy National Museum, New Delhi.

4

5. Head-hunter with *dao*.
More powerful and energetic
than several other figures in this
genre this image wears the
tattoo marks and the necklace
characteristic of a head-hunter.
Coll : National Museum,
New Delhi.
Photo : courtesy National
Museum, New Delhi.

5

suggested by grooves and occasionally, two rows of incised teeth are shown in the mouth. Ear decorations consisting of dyed hair, seeds, and coloured cotton are stuck imaginatively to the wooden head to enhance its awesome appearance.

In many heads tattoo marks are prominently drawn with black paint on the forehead, the cheek, and the chin. The tattooing pattern on the face generally consists of painted continuous parallel lines running over the eyebrows and curving inwards over both cheeks towards the nose and then downwards to converge at the chin. Occasionally black tattoo dots are employed instead of the lines, and in some cases cover the entire face. Rarely does the tattoo motif assume the form of incised lines.

In most of the carved wooden heads, the faces are square with gentle demure expressions. Although some of these appear to be death-masks they show realistic characteristics. Such death-masks are devoid of tattoo marks for the tattooed face reflects the seriousness of the head-hunter's purpose and is fraught with power. This is particularly noticeable in the multiple heads carved on the single block of wood. Panels with multiple heads are usually found in a single row numbering two to five. There are, besides, a few specimens portraying small supplementary heads on the top of unusually elongated foreheads. They are reminiscent of crowns found among Buddhist tribes. Twin heads are often carved on both sides of a piece of wood.

Grave Effigies

Grave effigies as found among the Wanchos and the Konyaks are simplistic representations of human figures. Generally, an effigy is in the form of a wooden post, the upper portion of which bears a crudely painted human face while the lower portion is marked by some anatomical details. Occasionally, grave effigies are decorated with earthly possessions of the dead person such as ornaments, textiles, and baskets. The grave effigies are so simplistic in their execution that often it is impossible to determine whether it represents a male or a female. Unlike the head-hunter's replicas these objects have a grim appearance and this, together with their

6. Head-hunter.
While sculpting this figure the artist has emphasized frontality and solidity. The execution is carried out in flat planes without much attempt at delineating the contours of the body.
Coll: National Museum, New Delhi.
Photo: courtesy National Museum, New Delhi.

7. Head-hunter figure with a snake motif.
The coiled snake on the chest of the figure indicates connections with the regional fertility cults.
Coll: National Museum, New Delhi.
Photo: courtesy National Museum, New Delhi.

6

7

29

8

9

10

8. Four seated figures.
Inspired by the *morung* traditions of carved pillars, this piece portrays four seated persons on a platform. Below are a number of small dancing figures. This charming sculpture is devoid of any religious significance.
Coll: National Museum, New Delhi.
Photo : courtesy National Museum, New Delhi.

9. Seated figure.
This rotund secular figure has a contemplative expression which is in striking contrast to the triumphant expressions of the fierce head-hunters.
Coll: National Museum, New Delhi.
Photo : courtesy National Museum, New Delhi.

10. Addorsed figures.
This unusual sculpture apparently depicts a head-hunter standing with his victim – in this example, a woman – absorbing its *mana*.
Coll: National Museum, New Delhi.
Photo : courtesy National Museum, New Delhi.

11. Tasselled figure.
Carved images of the head-hunter's cult stand apart from the rest in iconography.
Coll: National Museum, New Delhi.
Photo : courtesy National Museum, New Delhi.

12. Head-hunter with painted tattoo marks.
This figure bears on its face and chest tattoo designs typical of the Naga head-hunters.
Coll: National Museum, New Delhi.
Photo : Datta Gupta.

13. Grave effigy of a head-hunter.
Melancholic faces are characteristic of effigies of the dead fashioned in the north-eastern region. The summary treatment can be attributed to their temporary importance. After the requisite rituals have been conducted, the figure is left untended and disintegrates.
Coll: National Museum, New Delhi.
Photo : Datta Gupta.

14. Head with black varnish and attached yellow fibre string.
Coll: National Museum, New Delhi.
Photo : courtesy National Museum, New Delhi.

15. Head with tattoo marks.
The blue beaded eyes and ear decorations impart a lively expression to the image.
Coll: National Museum, New Delhi.
Photo : courtesy National Museum, New Delhi.

16. Beer mug.
Used by Naga chiefs the mugs are carved and painted. The decoration in high relief includes the figure of a head-hunter and a *mithun* head.
Coll: National Museum, New Delhi.
Photo : courtesy National Museum, New Delhi.

12

13

14

15

16

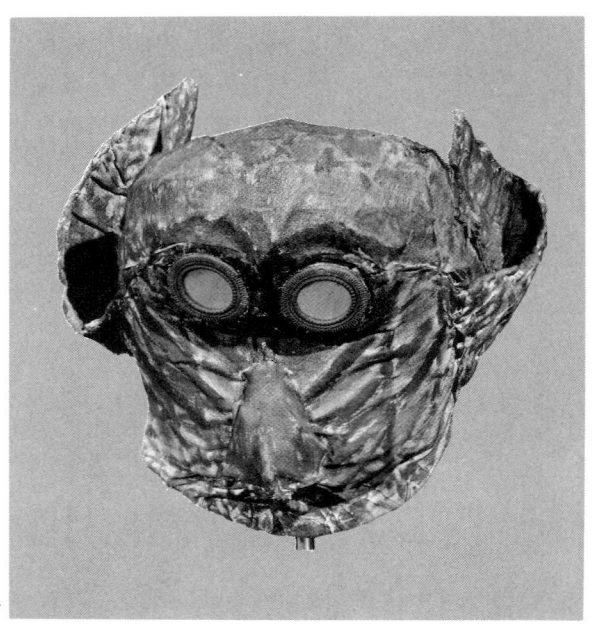

Masks.
Used in Buddhist festival dance performances, these masks portray animal and human heads.

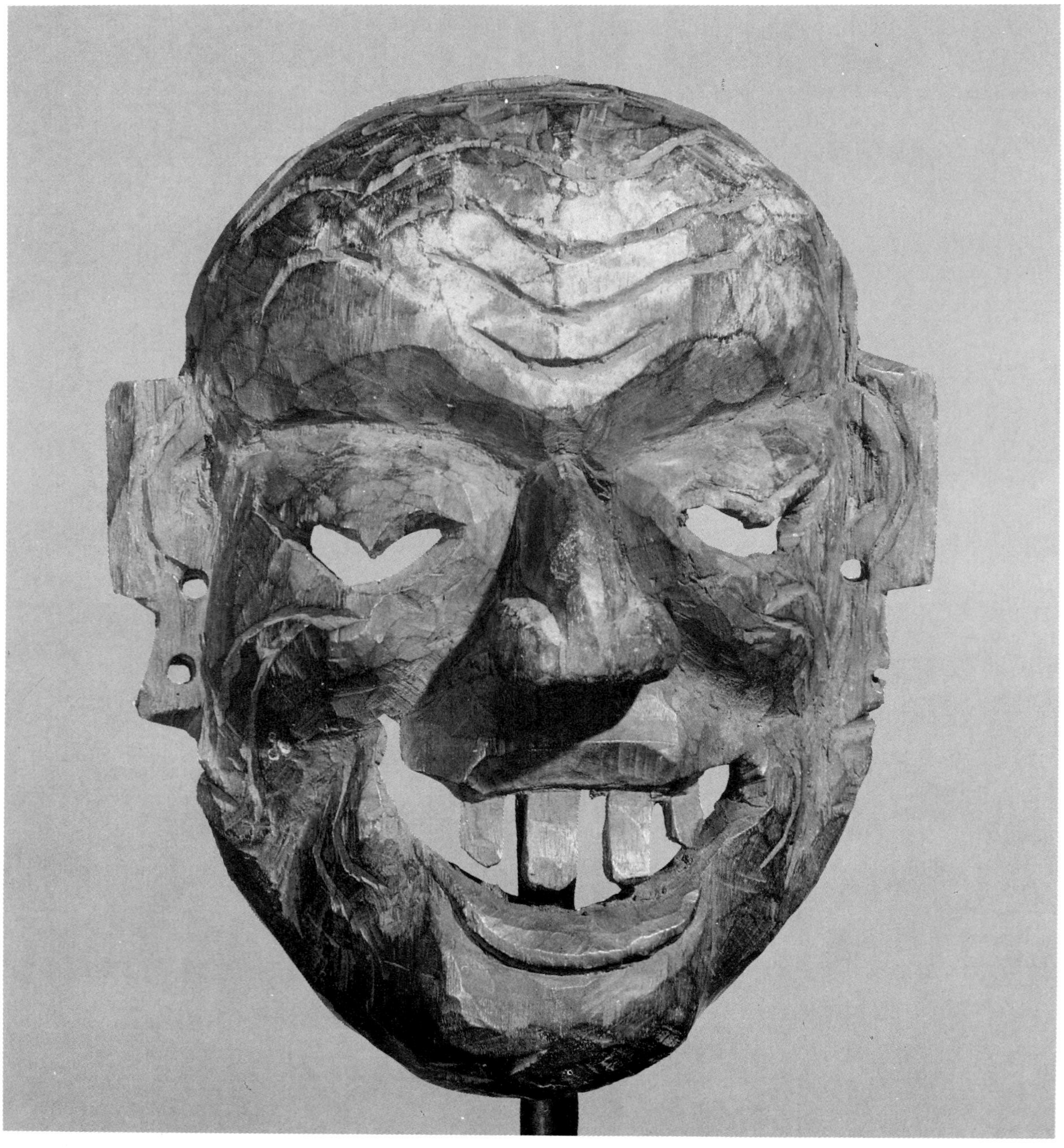

17. Animal head.
A mask made of cloth stretched on a bamboo frame. Mirrors have been used for eyes.
Coll: National Museum, New Delhi.
Photo : courtesy National Museum, New Delhi.

18. Head of a cock.
Made of tin, this mask is executed and painted realistically.
Coll: National Museum, New Delhi.
Photo : courtesy National Museum, New Delhi.

19. Wooden mask depicting a caricatured face.
Such masks are employed in Monpa dance performances.
Coll: National Museum, New Delhi.
Photo : courtesy National Museum, New Delhi.

20. Animal-face mask.
The unusual patterned execution and snarling mouth impart ferocity and character to this carving.
Coll: National Museum, New Delhi.
Photo : Datta Gupta.

17

18

19

Textiles and ornaments.
Woven by women on small loin looms the textiles reveal geometrical patterns executed in weave or embroidery. The ornaments are varied and are often distinctive to each tribe.

21

22

21. Naga black, white, and red striped cloth.
Coll: National Museum, New Delhi.
Photo : courtesy National Museum, New Delhi.

22. Naga red and white striped skirt cloth.
Coll: National Museum, New Delhi.
Photo : courtesy National Museum, New Delhi.

sketchy style clearly differentiates them from the cult figures. Frequently, these grave effigies, portray two figures side by side: it is believed that one of the figures represents the deceased while the other is his companion, male or female, to the other world. Sometimes, the effigies are signified by a mere piece of wood bearing a crudely painted face in black outline.

Verrier Elwin, during his researches in this field in the 1950s, had surmised that since grave effigies are produced at short notice they tend to be simplistic in their treatment of the anatomy as well as the face. This, in fact, is an erroneous belief, because among the Naga tribes, the mortuary rites continue for a long period and are carried out in successive stages. Therefore, it is not imperative for the effigy to be made right at the beginning of the ceremony, it can be fashioned during one of the many stages of the ceremony. Thus, the carver is not constrained by lack of time. Rather, the style appears to be specific to the occasion of death.

Morung Carvings

The *morung* is a dormitory for young men and is a shed with beams, pillars, and a thatched roof. The pillars and beams are profusely carved in low relief. The *morung* doors are also embellished with carving. The *song-kong* (a log drum), an essential feature of the *morung,* is ornamented with carvings.

The *morung* wood carvings are executed artistically and are admired greatly. They consist of free-standing images as well as engravings of animal figures and geometrical symbols. Tigers, lizards, and *mithun* (bison) heads are popular motifs. The hornbill is featured often. Among the free-standing sculptures certain motifs appear frequently: a man in a typical sitting posture, a dancing couple, dancing girls, and a woman combing the hair of a man.

The older Naga wood carvings show an affinity to wooden sculptures from Java and Borneo. The similarity in style can be ascribed to the radiations of art traditions from the South-East Asian countries to north-east India with the early tribal migrations. Curiously, the influence in the case of tribal art came to India from South-East Asia unlike classical Hindu art where the tradition flowed from India to South-East Asia. Unfortunately, the exposure to the outside world has led to the dilution in quality in the art of *morung* wood carving.

Masks: A Trans-Himalayan Legacy

The Buddhist tribes use masks for dance and pantomimes. This custom can be traced to the sixteenth century when the monks from the Towang monastery, established in the Kameng district of Arunachal Pradesh, propagated Buddhist philosophy in this region. A large number of dances, in the trans-Himalayan style, are regularly performed during Buddhist festivals and ceremonies.

Masks were also integral to the magico-religious practices prevalent in this region among the different tribes. Dance performances with masks for recreation and amusement are common in the Kameng district of Arunachal Pradesh. They are also prevalent in the Kamlang River valley, in the Lohit district of the same state. These dances are secular in nature; their themes draw inspiration from local folklore and also include erotic expressions. The masks are used for characterization. The tribals thus, create masks for elucidating Buddhist philosophy, for magico-religious rites and rituals as well as for secular entertainment.

Both the deer and the yak dance express concern for the environment in Buddhist philosophy. They emphasize the protection of nature and the need for human compassion towards animals. The destruction of evil by the forces of nature is symbolically depicted in the *jachunaga-chham* dance where the cosmic force is represented by a terrifying man-eating bird. The mask depicting this divine bird, with its imposing horn, projecting eyes, and menacing beak, is artfully executed. In another identical pantomime, the story tells of two benevolent bird spirits who have saved human beings from venomous reptiles. The mask depicting one of the benevolent bird spirits shows round bulging eyes, a menacing beak, two horns, a stylized head decoration, and the use of contrasting colours.

Entirely different from the stylized wooden masks discussed above are the demon masks of the *ajlamu* dance of the Sherdukpan tribe and other similar masks used by the Monpas of the Towang area. Since these masks do not conform to the conventional Pan-Himalayan style, they are, in all probability, manifestations of a pre-Buddhist era. The use of cowrie shells in both types of masks points towards an earlier tradition and can be compared with primitive masks found elsewhere in India.

The masks connected with magico-religious practices of the Monpas and Sherdukpans are

23

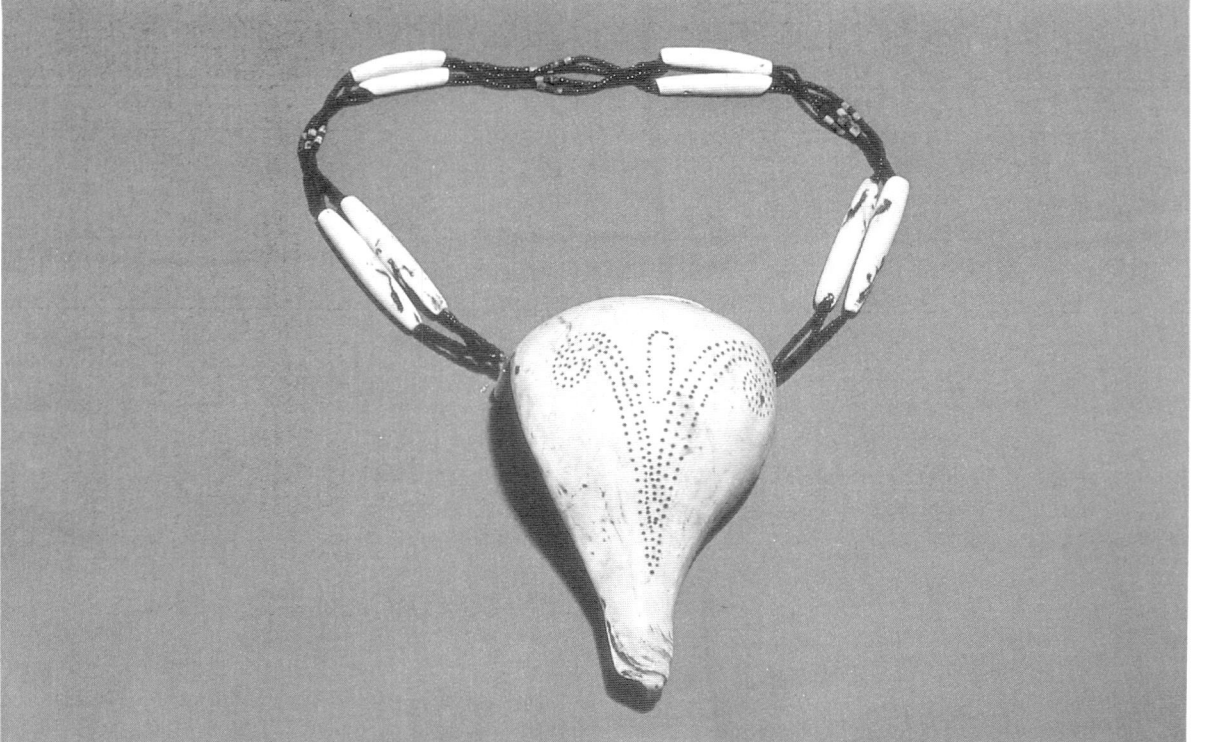

24

23. Bamboo basket.
Usually carried by head-hunters in a dance performance, this basket is decorated with a monkey skull, boar tusks, and squirrel tails.
Coll: National Museum, New Delhi.
Photo : courtesy National Museum, New Delhi.

24. Necklace with conch pendant.
Coll: National Museum, New Delhi.
Photo : courtesy National Museum, New Delhi.

even more realistic and concrete. They represent the frightening aspect of the demon divinity and are remarkably effective visually. The most common motif in this category of masks shows the deformed and diseased faces of human beings. With great skill the craftsmen have shown abnormal facial features such as squint-eyes, deep wrinkles, goitre, and cracked lips in as realistic a manner as possible.

Masks used in secular performances are quite comical in so far as their pre-Buddhist elements are concerned. The most notable are the masks worn by Arakacho and his wife – two popular figures in the pantomime of the Mankhota tribe in the northern Siang district of Arunachal Pradesh. Among the Memba tribe the secular demon masks are effective in stimulating fun and frolic among the spectators. Its pre-Buddhist background notwithstanding, all these masks conform to the style of the Pan-Himalayan tradition.

The masks and the mask-dances of the Khamti tribe do not portray the sophistication of the masks employed by the Monpa or Sherdukpan tribes. Their secular masks, such as the one used in the cock-fight dance usually performed to welcome guests, and the *phi-phy* masks representing ghosts and animal spirits are actually comical and display the ingenuity of Khamti artists. The animal masks made from yellow and black fabrics with small mirrors representing eyes belong to a very primitive style. The Khamti masks are crude and devoid of stylization and exaggeration. Unlike grotesque masks of the Monpa tribes, the Khamti masks are incapable of producing intense horrifying effects: in fact they are humorous and down to earth. The enlightenment of Buddha is the central theme in most of the mask-dances.

Textiles: Techno-morphic Art

Textile weaving is probably one of the more developed art-forms among the tribes of the north-eastern region. The use of bright and striking colours as well as varieties of geometric patterns make the textiles quite distinctive. The geometric patterns and their colour composition carry

25. Naga cap.
Naga men wear caps structured from bamboo strips dyed red and yellow and decorated with a boar tusk and *mithun* fur.
Coll: Dr Siddharth and Yashodhara-raje Bhansali.
Photo : Dr Siddharth Bhansali.

25

specific meanings and symbolic values which can be understood only in their particular socio-cultural context. Not enough attention has yet been paid to understand the meaning of textile motifs. Although the symbolism may vary from village to village and tribe to tribe, there is, undeniably, a general agreement in the interpretation of these motifs. Verrier Elwin was the first scholar to recognize this and he published their identification and meaning in 1959 in his book, *The Art of North-East Frontier of India*. The most commonly noticed geometric motifs are the diamond, zigzag, herring-bone, and the triangle. He also pointed out the presence of zoomorphic and anthropomorphic forms in certain textile patterns.

The motifs called *japapore* found in the textiles of the Adi tribes exhibit twelve different geometric shapes. The fabrics belonging to the Mishmi tribes are famous for their intricate multiple geometrical patterns. By contrast, the Apatani *ziliang* (priest's apparel) consists of curvilinear designs. The apparel of the Monpa and Sherdukpan tribes reveal a number of conventionalized motifs symbolizing various zoomorphic as well as floral forms. The textiles of the Wancho tribe are characterized by a three-dimensional effect achieved through the use of sharp contrasting colours and the use of thick woollen yarn over the white cotton base. The diamond patterns are generally outlined in green thread and deep red yarn.

Interestingly, the meaning attached to a particular symbol appears to be identical even among tribes that are widely separated and hail from a different cultural background. For example, the Apatani tribe refers to the diamond pattern as *aku* while the Nishi tribe calls it *anne*. Both the terms denote an eye. The Wancho and the Nocte tribes, further in the east, regard the diamond pattern in the same fashion and with the same conviction. This overall unity in form and content is again evident in the *redow* among the Apatanis and the *poppiir* of the Adis. Both represent the butterfly motif and are shown in the form of a crude cross. Similarly, the *tyada* motif, which occurs in the *ziliang* shawl of the Apatanis and the *tongmo* of the Adi *gale* (skirt) signify an arrow-head and assume an angular form.

Patterned textiles are found mainly in the lower Siang region among the Adis. The meanings attached to their textile motifs indicate an intimate connection between man and his physical environment. Geometric patterns such as straight lines and zigzag lines represent rivers, foliage, mountains, and other such aspects of nature.

Various geometric patterns woven on the *gale* (skirt) of the Adi tribe are collectively called as *pore* and are generally symbolic. A *pore* without any significance is known as *reku*. *Reku* compounds two morphemes – *pore* and *aku*. *Aku* means original while the syllables *po* and *re* stand for colour and pattern respectively. Hence the term *reku* denotes an original pattern. Apparently in the *reku* there is less emphasis on colour than in the *pore* patterns. We may assume here that whenever a pattern is deprived of its required colour scheme it becomes a non-symbolic *reku* pattern. Thus, it is clearly evident that the symbolic meaning of a particular design arises not only out of the techno-morphic shapes employed but also the colours that have been used.

Ornaments: Communicative and Symbolic

In 1926 a dispute was reported over the right to wear an ivory armlet by a particular Ao Naga clan and it shows the significance attached to ornaments by the tribal folk. Among the tribal communities ornaments are not mere items of personal adornment but have social, political, and religious connotations. In the north-east, as in various parts of India they are imbued with symbolic and communicative values.

As is the case of many tribal communities the ornaments in the north-east are made from items provided by nature such as seeds, bark, orchid stalks, cane strips, areca spathe, cowrie shells, conch shells, twigs, dyed goat's hair, as also claws, and teeth of bears, monkeys, or pigs.

Red seeds are used for making ear-plugs by the Noctes and Wanchos of Arunachal Pradesh as also the Konyak Nagas of Nagaland. Mention must be made here about the Kabui Naga ear decoration made of reed stalk dyed yellow or blue. Wooden cylindrical pieces blackened by a natural process are used as nose and ear-plugs by the Apatani women. A cane strip dyed red along with the yellow orchid stalk are appended to a conical hat and this is often accentuated with the tusk of a wild boar. Apatani cane waistbands dyed red are distinctive objects of art. Cowrie shells are generally studded in cane and leather waist belts. Conch shells often decorate the bead necklaces of the Naga tribes. Bark and areca spathes are used as headbands by the Wanchos and the Noctes. These headbands are embellished with a sort of poker-work – a technique by which the dried surface of the areca spathe is burned by using

26. Naga chief.
Clad in picturesque attire, this patriarch holds traditional attributes symbolic of his status. Photo: courtesy collection of the late Sumant Moolgaokar – Padma Bhushan.

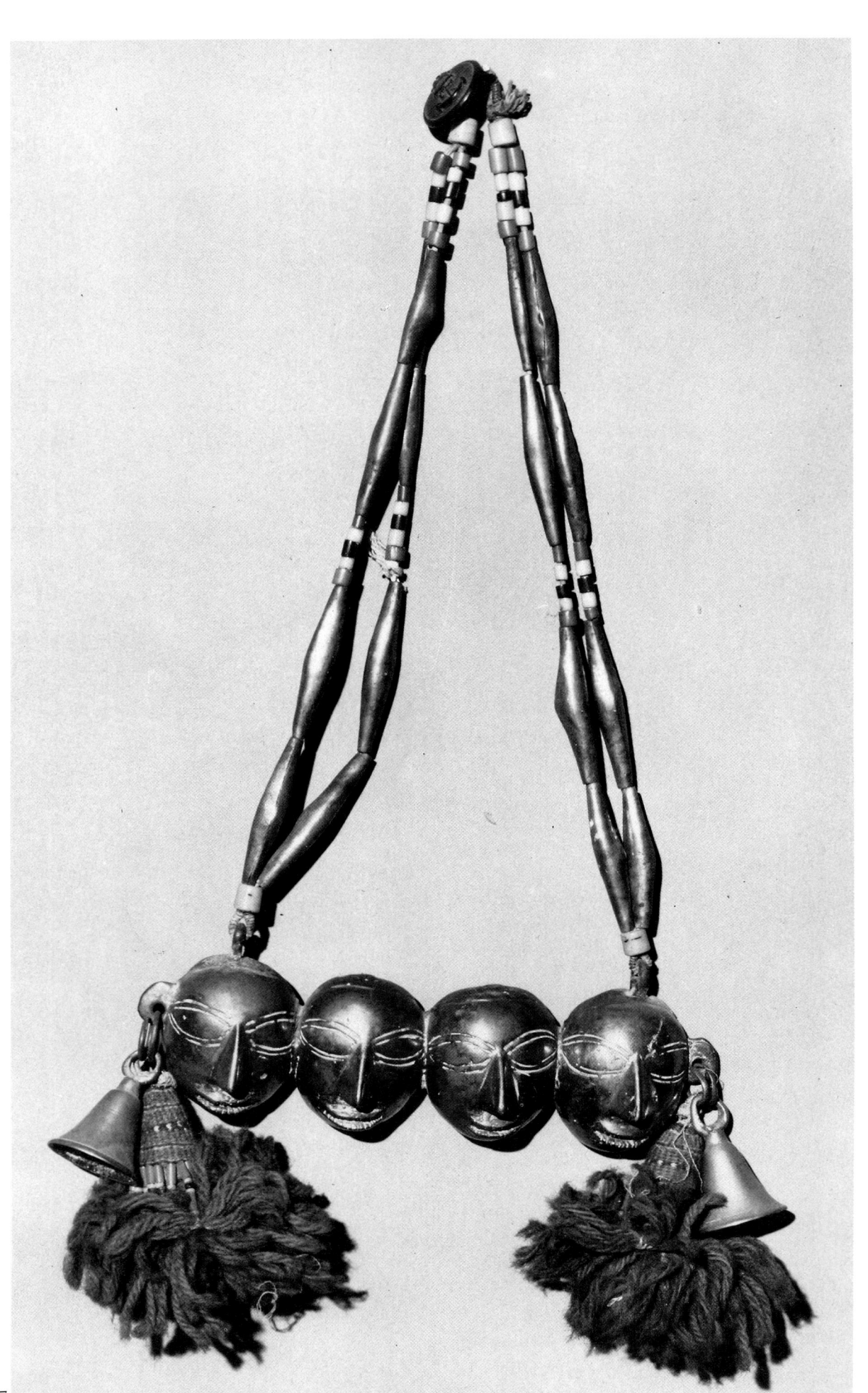

**27. Head-hunter's necklace
with four brass heads.**
Coll: National Museum,
New Delhi.
Photo : courtesy National
Museum, New Delhi.

28. Head-hunter's trophy.
A bead necklace with a wooden
human head pendant.
Coll: National Museum,
New Delhi.
Photo : courtesy National
Museum, New Delhi.

27

a hot iron needle – the motifs being human and animal figures.

In Naga society, a boy receives his first ornament at the age of seven or eight. At this stage he wears a thick brass arm band called *khanshiri*. This he discards when he obtains the right to wear the *shipu* (boar-tusk necklace) by making payment to the village elders. In a similar fashion the Adi girls are given a brass disc waistband which is replaced by a more elaborate band called *beyop* made of buffalo hide and round brass discs after the puberty ritual. *Lakap* or conch shell necklaces are generally worn by a man of a high social position. The conch shells are cut into several pieces and are used together with now rare bone-beads.

The most striking ornament among the Konyaks, Wanchos, and Noctes is the head-hunter's necklace. Made of brass it has three or five pendants in the form of human-heads. The heads are cast by a primitive method – the eyes and the nose are indicated by crudely incised lines. These brass heads actually come from the Kachin area across the Patkoi range in Myanmar. Occasionally, coral beads are put along the brass locket.

Various Naga groups such as Sema, Lotha, Angami, and Ao wear above the elbow a heavy cylindrical ivory armlet with incised decoration called *khambang*. The right to wear it is strictly defined: some clans are entitled to wear only a single ivory armlet, while others can wear a pair, and some clans can earn the entitlement only after sacrificing a *mithun*.

The bead necklaces, headbands, waistband, and arm bands of the Wanchos, Noctes, and Konyaks display superb taste in the way in which small glass beads are entwined in a network of geometric patterns and colour compositions. In the necklaces or waistbands used by the members of the chief's family human motifs are inserted.

Among some communities of lower Siang in Arunachal Pradesh, the value of a particular ornament is based on socio-religious norms. One such specimen is an *emule* or *mulli* belonging to the Padams of the Adi tribe. The *emule* is made of a single metal disc approximately four inches in diameter with triangular projections at the rim and a knob in the centre. It is tied with a tassel which is called *ridin*. The tassel is made from the creeper of the same name with a bead tied at one end. It is customary for the hunter to wear an *emule* as a talisman after killing a tiger. It is believed that the *emule* protects the hunter from the spirit of the tiger. Also, it is worn by a person who survives an accident as a protection against recurrence of a similar incident. The *emule* is believed to possess supernatural powers; it cures men of illness and its efficacy is increased if it is given by the maternal uncle.

In this region it is customary to pass on ornaments as heirlooms from mother to daughter, and father to son. *Dudap* is an ornament which is inherited either by the eldest or the youngest son. This necklace is generally found in possession of the more prosperous families. It is one of the most coveted necklaces of the Adis of Arunachal Pradesh. The *dudap* consists of nine different parts made of different materials such as *tatick* (bone buttons), *lori* (black beads), *angnuk* (glass beads), *gumpun* (white glass beads), *gunmet* (turquoise pieces), *elong* (ivory pieces), *pishic* (brass plates), *gumka* (black beads), *ponguk* (blue glass beads), and *demmur* (red woven tassel). These pieces display great beauty, skill, and imagination in the manner in which they combine beads of different materials and colours as well as other objects such as ivory, bone, and brass plates into one single ornament.

The art of the north-east Indian tribes has to be viewed as an aspect of its various socio-religious systems rather than as a deliberate and conscious search of beauty by the tribal artist for art's sake. Its art-forms are reproductions of standardized format in style, media, and technique fixed by an age-old tradition. Art here, consequently, is not a flight into the realm of emotion and fantasy, but lies in the plane of the common human pursuit of existence, profane and sacred. It is utilitarian in motive and derives its appeal from its supposed efficacy in promoting a useful purpose in life.

FURTHER READING
1. Mills, J.P. *Ao Naga*. Oxford University Press, Delhi, 1973.
2. Elwin, Verrier. *The Art of North-East Frontier of India*. North-East Frontier Agency, Shillong, 1989.
3. Read, Herbert. "Art in Aboriginal Society: A Comment." *Artist in Tribal Society*, edited by Marion Smith. Routledge and Kegan Paul, London, 1961.
4. Das, A.K. "A Special Treasure." *India Magazine*, vol. 10. New Delhi, May 1990.

SABITA RANJAN SARKAR

BENGAL

As many as thirty-eight tribal communities inhabit Bengal and are at present distributed in different parts of the state. On the basis of their ethnological character, their original homeland, their routes of migration, and their current distribution pattern, the tribal communities of Bengal can conveniently be divided into three broad culture zones:

1. Mongoloid tribal communities such as the Lepcha, Bhutia, Toto, Garo, Mech, Rabha, and others are concentrated mostly in the hilly and jungle areas of Bengal. The Lepcha, and the Bhutia who have migrated from Sikkim, Bhutan, and Tibet live predominantly in the hill tracts of Darjeeling district.

2. The Garo, Mech, and Rabha who have migrated from Assam have settled down in the jungle clad Tarai region of the Jalpaiguri and Cooch Bihar districts.

3. The Dravidian tribal communities like the Oraon, and the Santal have emigrated from the Chota Nagpur plateau and now live in the remaining districts in the plains, such as Malda, Birbhum, Burdwan, Midnapur, and Purulia.

Wall-painting

Wall decoration, a salient feature of tribal art, is almost exclusively confined to the Dravidian tribes of the plains and is encountered primarily among the Santals. The paintings exhibit associations with regional ecology as well as the socio-economic life, religious beliefs, and the aesthetics of the Santals.

Wall embellishment is carried out by the females of the community starting from the procurement of natural ingredients of colour as well as their preparation and application. The colours are applied on the wall with indigenous brushes or pieces of cloth or the fingertips depending on whichever method is convenient.

The painting on the wall begins with the annual harvest festival *Soharai* which falls in the month of Kartik (October-November) when the rainy season is over and fair weather prevails. In this season people find adequate time for indulging in leisure activities. At the time of this festival, the floors and walls of the huts are repaired, and they serve as the canvas on which a series of motifs is painted. The walls are painted with just plain colours or decorated with geometric patterns such as triangles, quadrangles, parallel and wavy lines or motifs such as flowers, leaves, animals, birds, and fish. Floral designs are by far the most common. The flowers and leaves are stylized and somewhat abstract in form and shape and so are the animals such as the elephant, the tiger, and the serpent. Daily activities are shown – bird trapping and hunting of animals such as the boar, and the deer with javelins as well as the bow and arrow. Social life is not neglected. The paintings show group dances with drummers, musicians, and dancing girls holding hands. Occasionally, these portray a bridal procession with palanquins, bridal couples, and spectators. Among the recreational activities there is a preference for depicting cock-fights. The execution is precise and lively.

2

1. Bhutia mask.
The Bhutias have made their home in the hill tracts of the Darjeeling region. Of Mongoloid origin, they seem to have migrated to this area from Bhutan, Sikkim, or Tibet. The Bhutias practise Buddhism and like other Buddhist tribal communities of the region they perform the ritual "Devil Dance". The masks prepared for this purpose are made of wood and are quite colourful.
Photo: Sabita Ranjan Sarkar.

2. Santal village.
Situated in lush surroundings, the mud plastered huts decorated with wall-paintings reflect the Santal tribal ethos.
Photo: courtesy and copyright Jyoti Bhatt.

3, 4. Painted scrolls.
A group of painters known as *chasi patuas* prepare scrolls depicting scenes from Santal mythology, and scenes of Santals feasting and dancing. They are prepared for tribal clients whose tastes have been somewhat modified because they live in areas where there is considerable contact with the outside world.
Chester and Davida Herwitz family collection.
Photos: courtesy Mr and Mrs Chester Herwitz.

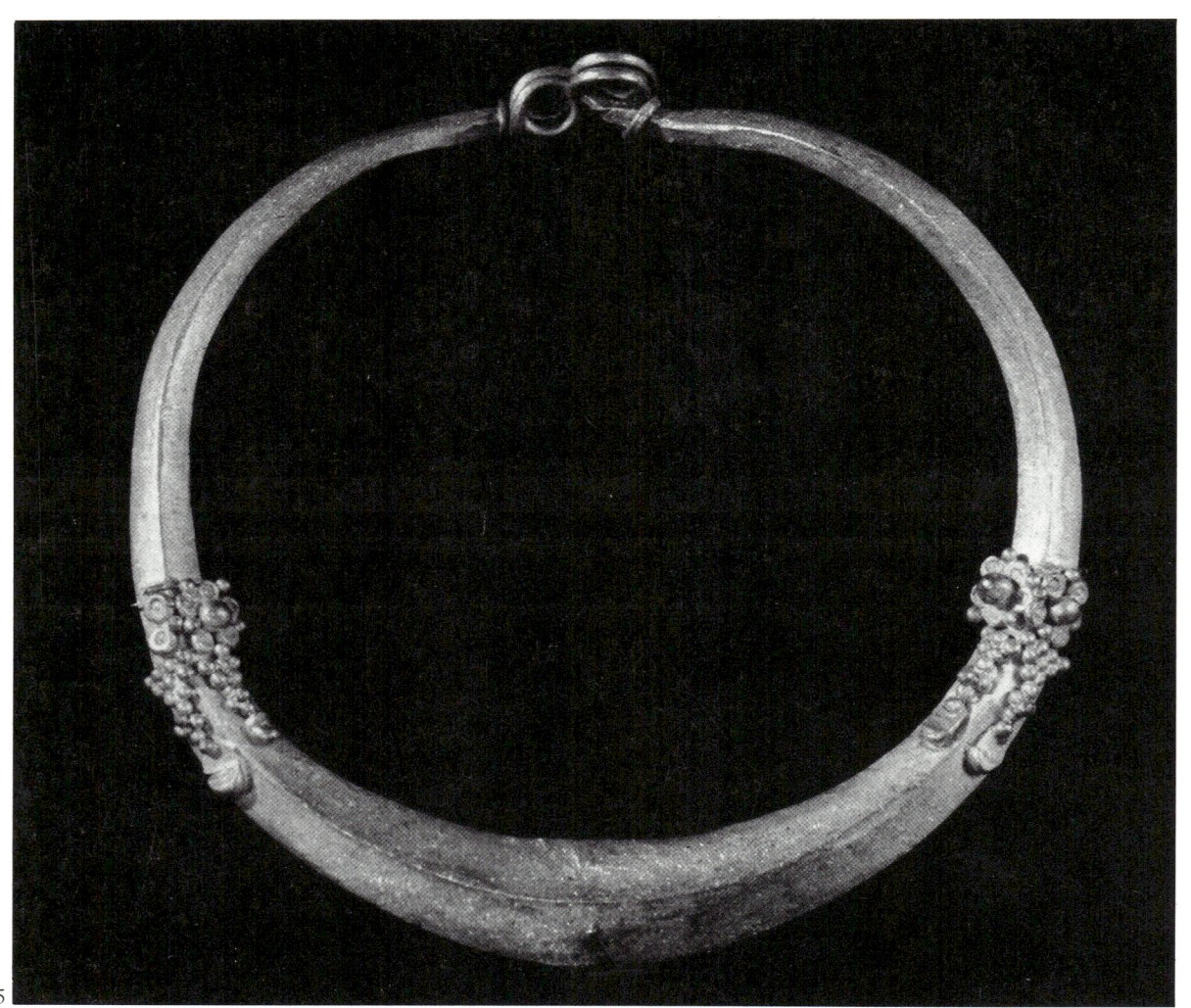

5. A metal neckband.
Photo : Sabita Ranjan Sarkar.

6. Bhutia necklace.
Photo : Sabita Ranjan Sarkar.

7. A jungle Rabha woman.
Photo : Sabita Ranjan Sarkar.

Apart from paintings, the walls of the Santal houses are sometimes decorated with sculptures in low relief. They portray animal forms, particularly cattle, birds – with a preference for the lively peacock, cock, and pigeon as well as floral patterns. The tribal artists generally try to give a realistic touch to their relief work.

With the change of the cultural environment of the tribals the subject-matter of their paintings is different. Instead of the tribal with the traditional bow and arrow, the "Saheb" hunter with a hat on his head and a gun in his hand, cars, buses, and lorries, which are now a familiar sight for the tribal also find a place in the paintings.

The traditional environment of the tribal living in the plains changed after the penetration of outsiders in large numbers. The introduction of better communication facilities as well as the establishment of rigid government controls over forest lands which were earlier freely enjoyed by the tribals have also played a part in disturbing the existing cultural patterns. Gradually, the tribals began to lose interest in decorating their huts with paintings. And since wall-painting was primarily an aesthetic exercise rather than a ritual event, there was no serious attempt at preserving this art-form.

Ironically, the situation worsened in the post-Independence era when the tribals were incorporated as a political force into the mainstream of Indian culture. The wall-paintings on the mud walls of the hut are now replaced with political slogans and posters. The walls now serve as a vehicle for political propaganda instead of aesthetic expression; fortunately, in remote areas, where the impact of modern culture and politics has not yet been felt keenly, the women continue to paint gaily on their mud hut walls.

Scroll Painting
Patas
Another kind of painting is associated with the culture of the Santals. The subject is related to the beliefs and ideas of the Santals. But the painting is prepared exclusively for the tribe on paper by a section of painters known as *jadu patua, jangli patua,* or *duari patua.*

The Santals believe that after death a man wanders aimlessly in the other world because of

8. A woman weaving.
The Mongoloid tribes usually weave their own fabrics which are colourful and decorated with different designs. The cloth is woven from cotton cultivated by them on small tracts of land.
Photo : Sabita Ranjan Sarkar.

50

the loss of eyesight. This eyesight can be restored by the *chakshudan* (granting eyes) ceremony. In accordance with this belief the *duari patua* is invited to the house of the deceased. The painter brings with him a stylized protrait of the man which is complete except for the irises of the eyes. In exchange for a little money or rice, the artist paints on the spot, the irises in the blank eyes. In this way the deceased man receives his eyesight and overcomes blindness. Hence the *pata* (folio) is known as *chakshudan pata* or *jadu pata*.

Later, the *jadu patuas* to improve their economic condition, began to include other subject-matter in their *patas*. They incorporated scenes of Santals feasting and dancing *(dangay* – the collective mixed dance after the hunting festival) as well as illustrations from their folklore and their deities such as the Baghut-Bonga (tiger god). The jungle environment was also portrayed. The *chasi patuas* prepared scrolls depicting Santal legends for their clients living in areas where the contact with the outside world was at its most intense.

Thankas

Among the Buddhist Bhutias of north Bengal, sacred *thankas* are prepared on Buddhist religious themes.

Jewellery

The tribals of Bengal are fond of ornaments. All the Dravidian tribes inhabiting the plains use more or less similar types of ornaments. The simplest form is a necklace made of beads, dry seeds, or fruits prepared by the tribals themselves and are still found on aged ladies in the interior areas. The taste, however, is changing in favour of metallic ornaments. But since they do not know the technique of making such ornaments, they are dependent on the local artisans for their supply. Earlier massive bracelets, armlets, and anklets of bell-metal were very common, but now the tribals prefer ornaments made of silver, plastic, or glass; they show a proclivity for floral designs. The tribal women adorn themselves with hairpins, ear-rings, nose-ring, rings, necklaces, armlets, bracelets, and anklets. Gradually, the tribals are moving away from their traditional jewellery towards the types worn by peasants in the region. This change can be traced to acculturation stemming from the opening up of tribal areas for economic development.

The ornaments used by the Mongoloid tribes in the hilly areas of Darjeeling district are different from those of the Dravidian tribes, both in the nature of the ornaments, as also in the constituent materials. The most popular ornament among them, is the amulet box made of silver and studded with turquoise and coral. Another popular item is the necklace made of beads such as cornelian, amber, coral, turquoise, jade, and even faience. These stones are obtained mostly from Tibetans. The bracelets and girdles reveal carved figures of deities and symbols with a distinct Tibetan influence. A simple silver necklace, locally known as *leyap* is an ornament for regular use among these tribes.

The jungle Rabhas of the Tarai region use both the metallic and the beaded ornaments. The girdle worn at the waist is a typical beaded ornament. Necklaces made from coins (common among the Assam tribes) are popular. They also use hairpins, ear-rings, bangles, and combs made from metal.

Textiles

The Dravidian tribal communities in the plains do not know the art of weaving. Traditionally, they did not feel the necessity of elaborate garments due to the tropical climate. Both men and women used very coarse white cloth. *Sar*, the woman's cloth was provided with a narrow coloured border without any design. Their apparel was of the simplest form with minimum or no scope for artwork. The tribals procured the materials from the local artisans. Nowadays these traditional garments are replaced with commercially produced fabrics used by other people in the region.

With the Mongoloid tribes of north Bengal, however, the situation is different. Almost all the families weave their own garments and learning how to weave was mandatory for the women. Until a few years ago, these tribes had no access to the artisan communities for their clothing. They cultivated cotton in their fields, and wove their own textiles.

These traditional tribal textiles were not only colourful, but also decorated with different designs. In form, design, and colour scheme, the textiles of the Darjeeling tribes differ from those of the Tarai region. In fact, the dress of the former, with their distinctive long stripes and subdued colours, reveal the heritage of their motherland, Tibet. The textiles of the latter group exhibit in the geometric character of their design and the use of bright colours over a dark ground, an affinity with the tribes of north-eastern India.

The principal dress of the Bhutia and the Lepcha men of the mountainous Darjeeling area is a coat with overlapping flaps extending down to the knees. The women wear a blouse and a lower garment consisting of a cotton cloth wrapped around the waist like a skirt. The length of this garment varies. The tribes of the Tarai region such as the Rabha, Garo, and others wear a breast band, a waistband, and a short apparel extending from the waist down to the knee. During winter, both men and women wear a colourful coat. The garments of Mongoloid tribes in the mountainous as well as the Tarai regions are intricately woven, colourful, and artistic.

Owing to the abolition of *jhum* (shifting cultivation) and the prohibition of cultivation of forest land, the growing of cotton for weaving is dwindling in north Bengal and since commercially produced materials are now easily available in the interior region, these tribes, particularly in the Tarai region, have given up weaving, and their traditional costumes are being replaced with modern dresses. However, efforts are now being made at craft training centres to keep this art alive and adapt it to modern day requirements.

Masks

Some of the glorious examples of tribal art are masks. The jungle Rabhas in the Jalpaiguri district of the Tarai region employ three types of masks : each has a distinct name, is made of a different material from the others, and functions differently.

Char-gog

The simplest one, *Char-gog*, is prepared by plaiting bamboo strips in the form of a winnowing fan. Its entire upper surface is covered with a piece of white cloth for conveniently colouring the uneven surface. The mask is absolutely flat except for the nasal bridge, made with a piece of wood. The ears and the tongue are given concrete shape with goat skin. The remaining features—the eyes, lips, and teeth are painted on the white ground in black and red. The sun and the moon are shown symbolically on the forehead.

With its protruding tongue, large eyes, exposed teeth, and fierce expression, the mask represents goddess Kali. The Rabhas call it the mask of goddess Chandi, a fearful deity and believe that it exercises a spiritual influence. This mask is employed in *Char-kheleyee* a religious dance organized immediately after Kali puja for collecting contributions from the neighbouring villages for the annual festival. After the event, the mask is cut into pieces and thrown away in the river for fear of incurring the displeasure of the goddess. Since the dancer with the mask has to walk long distances to reach his destination and has to dance from door to door the mask is constructed of a light material (bamboo strips).

The villagers have to offer rice for organizing this ritual dance. Earlier each Rabha family could cultivate rice in their allocated forest land and harvest it in the month of Bhadra and Aswin (September-October). Thus, at the time of Kali puja in the following month they would have sufficient rice to entertain the dancing party with food and drink as also payment in kind. But ever since India became independent the situation has changed because the government has imposed strict controls over cultivation of forest lands. Only a few families are allowed to cultivate the limited plots of forest land, the majority of the jungle Rabhas have to work as landless forest labourers. The Rabha landowners have taken to cultivating a different variety of paddy which is harvested after Kali puja, with the result that the jungle Rabhas do not have a sufficient quantity of rice at the time of Kali puja to organize their traditional *Char-gog* masked dance. Thus, in the last few decades the mask has become a vestigial cultural artefact and elderly Rabha craftsmen prepare it only on special request.

Char-pagal

The *Char-pagal* mask in the form of a human face is used in the religious masked dance, to entertain the gathering during the Kali puja festival. Carved out of a single piece of wood, it is flat with crude carving indicating the nasal bridge, the bulging forehead, and the depressed eye sockets. Facial features such as the eyebrows, lips, and teeth are painted in black and red on the white ground'of the mask. There is a naive quality about this wooden mask which also has lost its importance in tribal culture. Nevertheless, its importance as a representative example of Rabha wood carving cannot be denied.

Maper-char

The mask, used in the *Mapar-basini* dance, is made of a gourd shell. The elongated cylindrical piece is open at both ends. The facial features are painted on the upper surface. This mask of

9. Sacred mask.
This mask represents a benign female deity. Its sacred character is established by auspicious symbols of the sun and the moon on the forehead. Made from a winnowing fan of plaited bamboo strips, the surface is covered with a white cloth and the features are indicated in red and black colour.
Photo : Sabita Ranjan Sarkar.

9

10, 11. Musical instruments.
Among the Dravidian tribals of
the plains, wood carving is
limited and is confined to
utilitarian objects such as door
panels, musical instruments, and
weapon handles.
Fig. 10 : coll. and photo:
Siddharth and Yashodhara-raje
Bhansali.
Fig. 11: photo: courtesy Sankho
Choudhuri.

10

a bear is for collecting contributions. The villagers willingly contribute to this mask dance in order to avoid incurring the displeasure of this fierce animal.

The masked dance-drama, *Chor-khele* among the Mechs, a tribal community in northern Bengal is enacted for entertaining people. But over the past few decades the pattern of recreation has changed considerably and this drama has lost its significance.

Wood Carving

Among the Dravidian tribes of the plains, wood carving is rather limited, and is primarily confined to decoration on utilitarian wooden objects. Wood carving is, therefore, generally found on door panels, musical instruments, weapon handles, wooden furniture, and palanquins. The carving is executed in high as well as low relief and features designs with animals, flowers, fish, and birds.

Carving is not widely practised among the tribes of the Tarai region either. Among the jungle Rabhas wood carving takes the form of masks and three human figures of ritual significance, representing the *choukidar* (watch-man) and the *bura* and *buri* (traditional guards). They are employed in the annual ritual *Tarangi* meant to drive away the evil spirit responsible for diseases. These figures are installed on the outskirts of the village in the belief that they will guard the village against the return of the evil spirits which have been driven out on the day of worship. The figure of the *choukidar* is new and is modelled on the concept of the *choukidar* who looks after the law and order of the village. Hence along with the *bura* and *buri*, the *choukidar*, with a gun in hand, has been incorporated.

The Rabhas themselves prepare these wooden sculptures in conformity with their religious beliefs. Such wooden figures are made every year immediately before the annual festival of the village. The figures are discarded immediately after the function, and hence their execution is casual and their features simplistic. Presumably, lack of much experience in wood carving and the non-availability of suitable tools for the purpose, stand in the way of executing fine modelling in the Rabha wood carving. In addition to these figures, their crude knowledge of carpentry confines the Rabhas to making mortars and pestles, wooden frames for drums, and a few other domestic articles used in daily life.

The woodwork of the Bhutias of Darjeeling consists of masks and a block used as a book cover. They also make trays, stands for religious books, and tables for individual family altars.

Terracottas

The artistic taste of the tribals is often reflected in their ritual objects. The Dravidian tribal communities such as the Santals, Oraons, and Mundas of the plains use terracotta figures of the horse, elephant, and the tiger as votive offerings. The tiger, a dangerous animal of the forest, is deified by the local tribals and both in sculpture and in painting it is referred to as *baghu bonga*. Terracotta figures of the tiger and the elephant are offered to the sacred tree of the village to appease the animal gods for safeguarding the local people from their attacks. This belief is also prevalent among the tribals of the forest belt, but with the shrinking of the forest tracts, these beliefs have lost much of their importance.

The votive terracotta figures are prepared by the Hindu traditional potters living in the tribal zone, in strict conformity with the tribal taste and requirements. The figures are small, abstract, and stylized in form. Many of the other tribes of northern Bengal whether from the hill tracts or in the jungle belts use terracotta figures.

Each one of the three distinct tribal areas of Bengal exhibits certain salient features in the zonal artwork. This specialization is the outcome of the aesthetic sense of the regional tribals, their techniques, and technology in production of the artwork, available raw materials, religious beliefs, social needs, economic life, ecological influence, and the influence of other cultures. Distinct Buddhist influence is found in the work of the tribals from the hill tracts of the Darjeeling district. The influence of tribes from Assam is markedly observed among the tribes of the Tarai region. While the Dravidian group of tribals belonging to the plains area are the bearers of traditional tribal artwork of the Chota Nagpur plateau of Bihar. On the whole, the tribal art of Bengal reveals regional speciality instead of a common art-form throughout the state.

S.K. MAHAPATRA

ORISSA

While Orissa's tribal art and culture share certain universal characteristics common to all pre-literate and primitive cultures, it has also certain special features determined by the historical circumstances of the region which is modern Orissa. In terms of experience this region remained fairly isolated from the sweep of invasions and the imperial traditions which to a large extent determined the cultural patterns in north India; it was also one of the last regions to come under British rule. This isolation, even as it retarded educational and economic development, also made possible for the retention of traditional cultural forms in a comparatively purer, undistorted, and original form. Moreover, it led to the evolution of a composite culture which is a remarkable continuum of classical, folk, and tribal elements. This is evident in several areas: for example, in the sphere of religion many scholars feel that the tribal origin of Lord Jagannatha at Puri is a distinct possibility; apart from prevailing legends which point to that, the anthropomorphic wooden figure of the deity, looking half-formed and incomplete resembles the human figures in wood made by the Kondh and Saora tribal communities. The concept of the Vedic Rudra and the Puranic Siva become transformed in rural Orissa to the village deity Mahadev and, in case of the Santals, to Maran-buru. In the performing arts the Chhau dance of Mayurbhanj exhibits elements that can be the clearly traced to the classical Orissi tradition, the local folk expressions, and the Santal tribal dances particularly the Dantha and the Dasain.

Orissa's tribal art possesses certain characteristics which are common to all primitive art. It is functional and utilitarian and is not the product of the leisured activity of a privileged group or class. It is neither created by a small élite, often resembling an exclusive priesthood, nor is it meant for vicarious enjoyment of a few who can pay for it. It is participative, communal, and integral to the process of living and dying. There is no distinction between high art and low craft. A dance number may have an expanding circle of participants as three generations join in at the unsparing call of the accompanying drum beat. An ordinary object such as a Juang comb or a Dongria Kondh tobacco pouch may have etchings which are intricately designed and laboriously carried out. Art is created as one goes through life engaged in different activities within the community. To an extent, therefore, it is conventional in its patterns and rhythms and does not emphasize the creative ego of the artist or his individual inspiration. Art creation is a largely unstructured, communal activity that gives the individual a sense of fulfilment as a member of the community. The emphasis is rarely on the inspired individual ego.

Beyond the family and the community is the world of ancestors, gods, and spirits. In fact, the ancestors have an intimate link with the living members of the community and it is a sin to forget them on festive or ritual occasions. The village is the "sacred soil of ancestors" who participate in the joys and sorrows of their lineage. Then, there are the gods – generally forming large pantheons – both benevolent and malevolent, who have to be appropriately appeased through "offerings", and their blessings invoked for group welfare. The offerings include sacrificial objects and verbal invocations along with appropriate rituals. The motivation behind art creation has thus two primary sources: one functional – creating or decorating objects of daily use, etching designs on combs, painting the walls, and weaving scarfs; the other – religious or ritualistic, meant to be part of the "offering" to gods and ancestors.

Orissa has sixty-two tribal communities which differ widely in terms of their numbers, degree of acculturation, level of economic and educational backwardness, and articulation of cultural self-image through oral literature (songs, tales, and myths of creation), performing traditions (songs and dances), and the visual arts. Having worked for nearly two decades in the field of oral poetry of the Orissan tribal, or what is better termed as "song-poems", this writer may venture a generalization that, as a whole, the Orissan tribes have a stronger tradition in the performing arts than in the field of visual arts. Among the latter the dominant activity is wall-painting, sacred and secular, as well as ritualistic and decorative. Some of the tribes do make exquisite fabrics for their own use but on a rather limited scale. They are very fond of adornments, some of which they themselves fabricate while others are made for them, in a symbiotic economic relationship, by the non-tribal people in their immediate neighbourhood. More common are the etchings, the carving on doors, windows, and tobacco pouches. Stone sculpture is also primarily for ritualistic purposes.

Sculpture

Sculpting in wood, stone or metal is not a very popular activity among the Orissan tribes except those done for ritual purposes. The doors and windows of the Santals often exhibit geometric patterns and designs of flowering creepers and animals. The windows of the Juangs have

1. Roof-tile with a female figure.
The Oraon and Gond tribes of Sundargarh and Sambalpur make roof-tiles with stylized human figures.
Photo : courtesy S. K. Mahapatra.

2. Wall-painting.
The Gadabas are renowned for painting the inside of their houses – ceiling and walls – with plain bands and patches of earth colours such as red, yellow ochre, and white. In this example, a certain advancement is indicated by the depiction of flowers and geometrical patterns.
Photo : courtesy and copyright Jyoti Bhatt.

3. Traditional dance.
The women, attired in saris distinctive to their tribal group, dance with grace and abandon at both celebrations and festivals.
Photo : courtesy Michel Sabatier.

4. Bejewelled Bonda woman.
Tribal women are extremely fond of ornaments and in some tribes the men too show a similar bias. An outstanding example of this predilection for adornments is the Bonda woman who wears a number of metal collars and necklaces of coloured beads that hang below the navel and which completely cover the upper part of her torso. She wears bangles, brass finger-rings, and a waistband of brass or iron links which clasps at the waist of her short garment. On her shaven head the Bonda woman wears strips or filets made from the leaves of the palmyra palm. The profusion of her ornaments contrasts with her scantily clad body.
Photo : courtesy and copyright Stephen Huyler.

4

sometimes intricate designs and carvings. The Kutia Kondhs carve their doors with stylized forms of birds and animals that border on the surreal. Other articles of daily use such as wooden containers, boxes, and beams of houses also have carved figures of human beings, birds, and animals. The Dongria Kondhs use large wooden poles, variously carved, as Dharani Pennu or the earth goddess. In each village one can come across such carved poles which are worshipped by the villagers. Sometimes they are found in the individual household of the comparatively affluent. The Meria pillar, to which the human victim used to be tied in the sacred ritual of sacrifice – lasting three days in earlier times – used to be a well-carved pillar with a small death-bird perched on top. This writer had seen such a pillar in an interior Kondh village nearly a decade ago. In recent times, however, it is a rather nondescript pillar to which the sacrificial animal is tied. The carvings now are becoming rarer, and the ritual is also becoming a simpler affair compared to the once elaborate drinking, dancing, feasting, and singing the invocation to the earth goddess, as also the ritual anointing of the Meria pillar. These were described by both Macpherson and Campbell in their reports to the British administration while working on the assigned job of putting an end to the "barbaric rite of human sacrifice in Kondhistan". The Meria ritual employs an elaborate invocation song which is a prayer to the earth goddess to bestow plenty of crops, ensure the good health of the community, and save it from the depredation of wild animals. The Meria invocation is thus reminiscent of a Vedic invocation. The Meria pillar and the Dharani Pennu pole are carved variously in different villages. The Meria sacrifice and the worship of the Dharani Pennu is common to both the Dongria Kondhs of Koraput district and the Kutia Kondhs of Phulbani district.

It is, however, the Juangs who excel in their etchings on combs which are of different shapes and sizes and made of either timber or bamboo. Their designs are intricate and represent a mix of ritualistic and secular objects. The variety and range of depictions of the objects is simply fascinating. This small primitive tribal group perhaps makes the finest combs in timber and bamboo in the whole of India. The human figures are stylized and so too are the figures of animals such as horses and elephants enclosed within spaces created by geometric designs.

Then, there are the figures of the village deities carved in wood which are seen at the entrances of Kondh villages. The deities are supposed to guard the village against attacks of disease and pestilence and are placed in a small make-shift hut. But they do not have any particular significance as sculpture. The Kondhs also carve designs and panels on wooden planks and pillars incorporating ritual symbols.

The Gonds of Mayurbhanj give different shapes to solid blocks of stones by cutting and polishing them, and by making deities out of them. Such menhirs representing village goddesses are placed at the base of a tree in the outskirts of the village and receive worship.

Terracottas

In terracotta, the Gonds of Sundergarh have a measure of excellence and they make stylized figures of animals and tall multi-layered lamps, besides exquisite pitchers, bowls, and other earthernware articles of daily use. The Oraon and Gond tribes of Sundergarh and Sambalpur make roof-tiles with stylized figures of human beings perched on them and *tulsi chauras* (square pots used for growing the scared basil plant) as votive objects. They also make *dolis* (palanquins) with the bridegroom and bride sitting inside as charming objects. Tribes such as the Santals, the Oraons, and the Hos also fabricate their earthern vessels, pitchers, and containers in different shapes and sizes.

Metalware

In metalware some of the tribes have excelled in the art of *dhokra* casting though it seems certain that they initially learnt it from their neighbouring blacksmiths. The Bhuiyans of Dhenkanal and the Gadabas of Koraput are now fabricating various functional objects such as measures for rice, bowls, and ritualistic objects with decorative motifs of birds and animals. They are, however, not as significant and rarely as large as some of the *dhokra* objects made by the Bastar tribals. Some of the Kondh *dhokra* castings are, however, quite significant as votive objects. They also cast men and women in various stylized forms.

Votive Objects

The various ritualistic objects carved in stone or wood and fabricated with clay or metal, are used on different occasions for worship. Almost all the sixty-two tribal groups have large pantheons of

Stone and wood.

Although some primitive examples do exist, sculpting in stone or wood is not very popular among the tribal communities of Orissa. Carvings consist of patterns incised in low relief on beams, windows, and doors of houses or in articles of everyday use such as boxes or combs. The designs are simple and feature geometrical or floral patterns. Occasionally they employ animal or bird motifs– sometimes verging on surreal renditions as among the Kutia Kondhs.

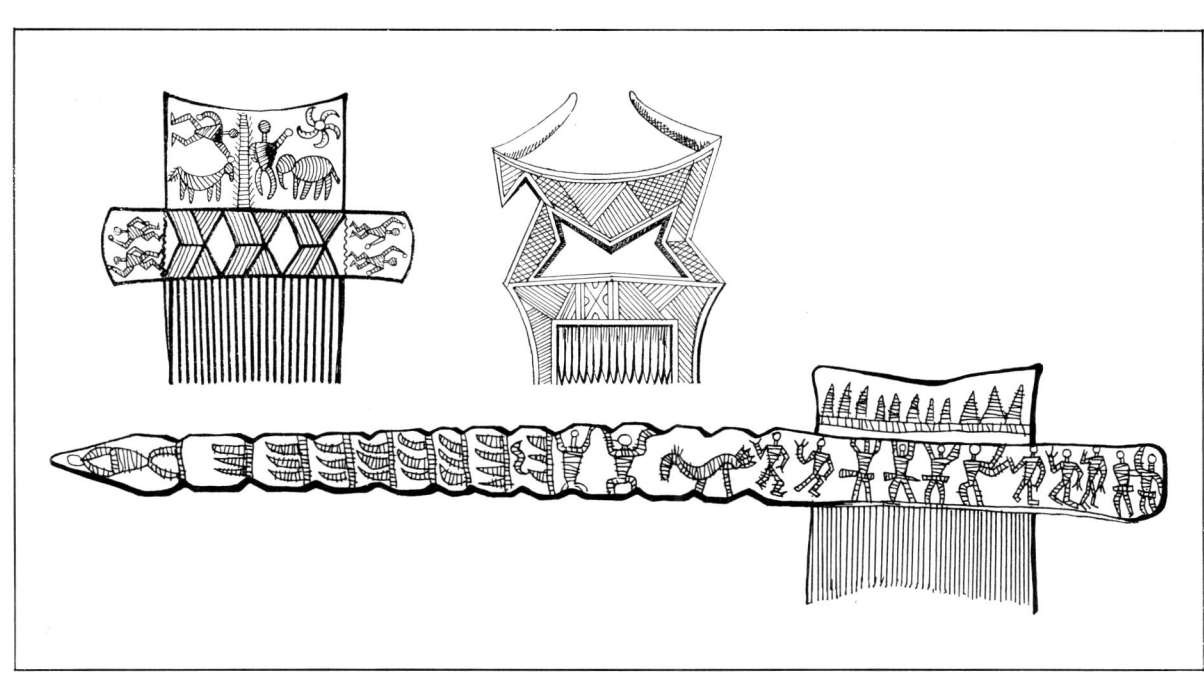

5-7

5, 6, 7. Juang combs.
The Juangs of Orissa excel at carving on combs of different sizes and shapes from timber and bamboo. Intricately etched, the designs combine secular and ritualistic motifs.
Line drawings : courtesy S. K. Mahapatra.

8. Palanquin.
The Oraons and Gonds make terracotta toy palanquins with the bridegroom and bride seated inside. This style adheres to conventionalized rendering and is prevalent in Bengal, Bihar, and Assam.
Photo : courtesy S. K. Mahapatra.

8

63

Metal objects.
The Bhuiyans of Dhankaral, the Gadabas of Koraput, the Dongria, and the Kutia Kondhs use metal objects for functional, decorative, and ritualistic purposes. The Kondh castings are significant as votive objects. They show men and women in stylized forms as also animal figures clothed in a tight-fitting web of wire mesh. This technique, though similar to that prevalent in Bastar, is coarser in treatment and less decorative in its effect. The essential difference between the two regional styles is that in the Kondh figures, the wires are laid in a mesh design, while in Bastar, they are laid parallel to one another.

9

10

9, 10. Animal figures.
Coll : National Museum, New Delhi.
Photos : courtesy and copyright National Museum, New Delhi.

11

12

11. A human couple.
Coll : National Museum, New Delhi.
Photo : courtesy and copyright National Museum, New Delhi.

12. Hunters seated on a machan.
Coll : National Museum, New Delhi.
Photo : courtesy and copyright National Museum, New Delhi.

13. An equestrian figure with attendants.
Coll : National Museum, New Delhi.
Photo : courtesy and copyright National Museum, New Delhi.

13

gods and goddesses, generally distinguished as malevolent or benevolent. Most of them are also animistic, recognizing trees, rivers, and hills as gods and making suitable offerings to them. In fact a very large number of votive objects in stone, wood, and metal answer the requirements of religious worship, both at the village level, performed by the priest, or at the family level, performed by the head of the household.

Textiles

In textiles, it is the Dongrias, the Gadabas, and the Santals who create a small range of exquisite designs on locally fabricated looms. The Dongria scarfs, which both men and women use to cover the upper part of the body, have exquisite traditional designs and a beautiful mix of colour. The Santal textile is more sophisticated in design and uses a larger range of coloured threads. The Gadabas mix cotton threads with the yarns made out of the bark of a local tree. Their sarees, with only two or three colour stripes, serve as the traditional dress of the women. The Bondas too, weave the tiny loincloth worn by the women on very small looms.

Jewellery and Ornamentation

The tribal communities of Orissa reveal a strong inclination to adorn their bodies with a variety of jewellery. The women are extremely fond of various types of jewellery and in some cases, as among the Dongrias, the men also show a predeliction for it. The most outstanding example of "heavy" jewellery is that of the Bonda women. The women with shaven heads have bare torso and wear only a very small and flimsy cloth loosely tied round the waist. But a large number of brass collars as many as seven in number and coloured beaded necklaces worn around the neck, hang below the navel and thus cover the entire upper part of the body. They also wear brass rings on their fingers and a waistband or girdle made of brass or iron links to keep the flimsy strip of loincloth in place. Round her shaven head the Bonda woman wears a number of bands of simple palmyra strips or woven and plaited filets. Into these bands the younger girls stick flowers and the older women their *bidis* (leaf-pipes). While the brass collars are purchased from local blacksmiths, the head-dress and the colourful bead necklaces are made by the Bondas themselves. The necklaces have coloured glass beads, shells, and beans and are mostly green, blue, ochre, and yellow in colour. The Bonda women also wear a number of brass bangles separated by rings of old cloth to prevent them from rubbing against each other.

The Dongrias are perhaps the most colourful when it comes to ornaments of both men and

Textiles.

In Orissa, the Dongrias, the Gadabas, and the Santals create a small but exquisite range of textiles on locally fabricated looms. These textiles portray sophisticated designs and employ a rich spectrum of colours.

14. Santal scarf.
Photo : courtesy and copyright Sankho Choudhuri.

15. Tribal women with draped woven textiles.
Photo : courtesy and copyright Stephen Huyler.

16, 17. Saora sacred pictographs.
In the Saora tribal community a pictograph is made during times of adversity, disease, and death. The ritual begins with the divination by the shaman who identifies the spirit that has caused the calamity and requires appeasement. The spirit is then invoked and by means of chantings and spells is invited to come and occupy the one dimensional temple that has been specially painted for it. The pictograph in effect serves as a means for capturing the spirit and imprisoning it in the ritualistic diagram. Such pictographs are drawn on the inner walls of the mud huts. Photos: courtesy S. K. Mahapatra.

Masks.
Wooden masks are employed in dance performances celebrating a successful hunting expedition. The masks portray highly stylized human and animal physiognomy.

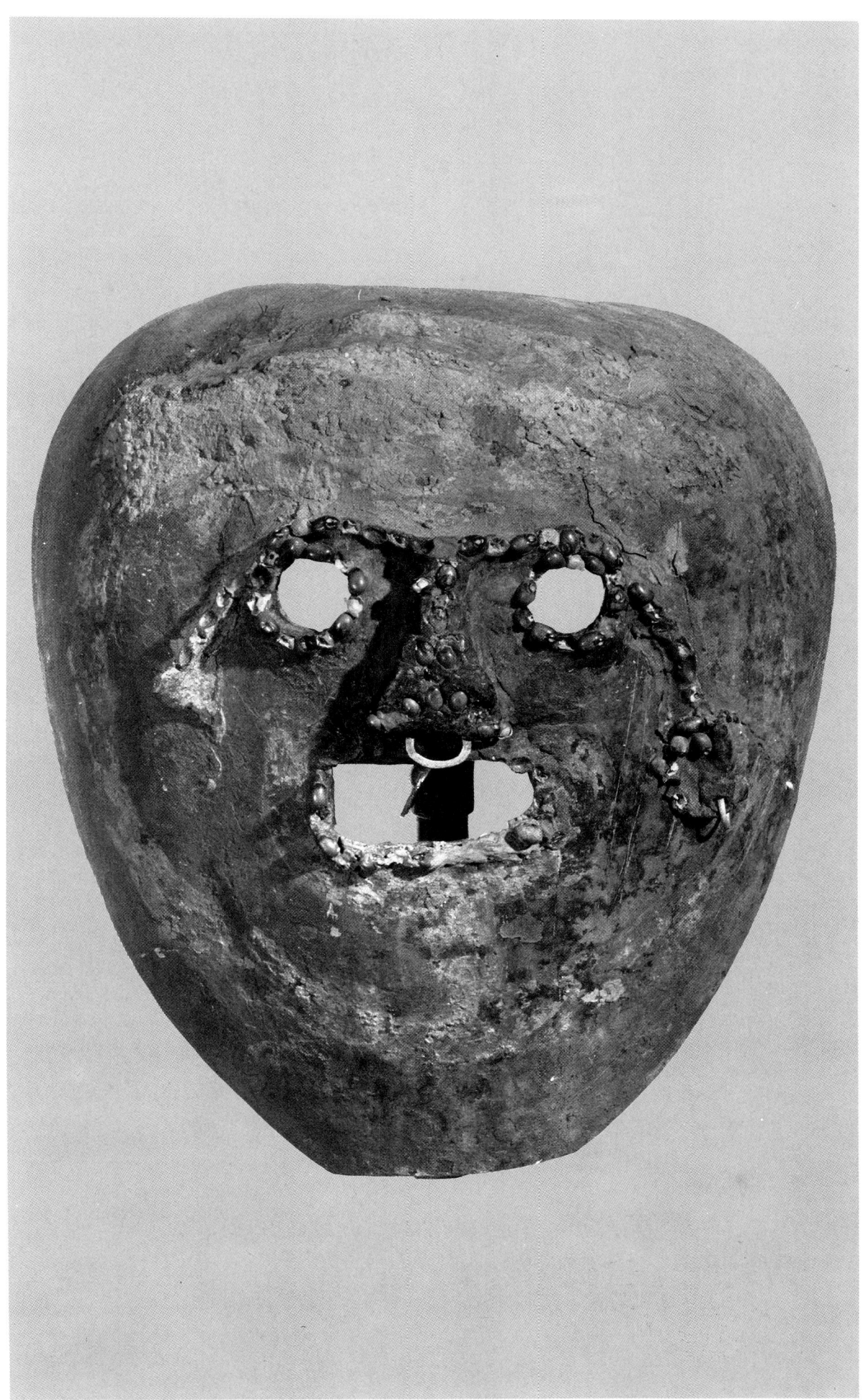

18. Human head.
Executed in an interesting manner the head has the eyebrows, nose, and mouth outlined with cowrie shells. The nose is also adorned with a nose-ring of metal.
Coll : National Museum, New Delhi.
Photo : courtesy and copyright National Museum, New Delhi.

18

19

20

women. While the Bondas generally do not wear ornaments on the nose and ears, Dongria men and women wear a large number of various types of rings on their ear lobes and nose. Their bead necklaces are also very beautiful with a fine blending of colours. The jewellery used by the Kondh women for their head is also exquisite, blending neatly with the dangling circular coins and the stylized coiffure. Among the Gadaba women's jewellery, apart from the necklaces of coloured beads, is a very large pair of ear-rings. Along with their sarees which they weave themselves, these bead necklaces and large ear-rings give a distinct look to the Gadaba women.

The Saoras, the Santals, the Parajas, and in fact, most of the tribal communities are inordinately fond of jewellery. Apart from necklaces of beads, the ornaments are made from humbler metals such as aluminium, brass, and sometimes copper. Necklaces of coins are also not rare and the Saoras even use wooden ear-rings.

Wall-paintings

Of the tribal communities in Orissa, at least seven have significant mural paintings on the mud walls of their houses. The Saora wall-paintings, which are popularly referred to as pictograms or icons have a ritual base. On the other hand, the wall-paintings of the Juangs, the Bhuiyans, the Dongria Kondhs, the Santals, the Gadabas, and the Gonds are more or less decorative in character and do not have any religious or ritual overtones.

Saora icon-making is related primarily to matters of good health and disease, epidemics, death, and childbirth. There are two distinct stages in this plastic art. In the first stage, the ritual divination by the priest leads to the identification of the "spirit" or the "power" that has caused a disease or death and that needs to be propitiated. It is at this stage that the words of the spell are used. Moreover, instead of an attempt to ward off the evil or malevolent spirit, here, the spirit is brought in or rather pulled or dragged in and installed and imprisoned in a ritualistic, one-dimensional temple on the icon painted on the wall.

The spell also has two sequences. In the first part, there is a general invocation to all gods and spirits that are supposed to inhabit the Saora world. In the second part, the particular spirit is invoked to come and occupy the house that has been specially made for it.

After the incantation has been recited and the icon drawn, either by the priest or the head of the household, is more or less complete, the artist makes a salutation to the god or spirit

19. Animal mask.
Abstract and attenuated, this angular rendering suggests an animal face, possibly a deer with a grave expression.
Coll : National Museum, New Delhi.
Photo : courtesy and copyright National Museum, New Delhi.

20. Human head.
This bold rendering is executed with short flat strokes. It is divided into three distinct strata. The hair-line and the teeth are simplified into grooved patterns, the eyes are indicated by small square holes, and the nose is not clearly demarcated as it gently nudges itself into the cheeks.
Coll : National Museum, New Delhi.
Photo : courtesy and copyright National Museum, New Delhi.

21. Mask.
With the facial features outlined in white, the mask has two straws which represent hair.
Photo : courtesy S. K. Mahapatra.

21

by touching the ground with his head and then recites the following before giving the final touches to the icon:

> "I have made a house for you. Here are your elephants, your horses. Come riding on them. Here are your suns and moons, crops and trees. Come and see what a nice house I have built for you with my own hands. Gods of the sky, come and see the house. Deities of the hills, come and see the house."

The Saora icons are drawn for the following purposes: generally satisfying the deities and ancestral spirits, averting any mishap including illness in the family, reaping a bumper crop, and improving the fertility of the soil, and ensuring easy childbirth.

The Saora houses are tiny structures with mud walls and thatched roofs. Very rarely, only if a man is somewhat rich, is the roof of tiles. Sometimes it is thatched with palm leaves. The mud walls are generally smooth though not as elegant or even as smooth and firm as the mud walls of Santal houses. The icons are drawn on the inner side of the walls of a house. The major icon is drawn on the wall close to the entrance of the house or on the wall facing the front door. In some houses, smaller icons are also drawn on other walls of the house. These smaller icons are invariably drawn in places where the eye cannot discern them as easily as those drawn near the front door. The Saora pictograms manifest a curious amalgamation of the traditional and the new. It is the product of an agricultural community with an emphasis on the sun, trees, water as well as ploughing and scattering of seeds. And yet, one also notices bicycles, automobiles, chairs and tables, confabulations and constructions – all the influence of the outside world impinging on their lives.

Unlike the Saora pictograms, the paintings and designs of the Santals, the Bhuiyans, the Dongria Kondhs, the Juangs, the Gonds, and the Gadaba tribes are decorative in nature and purpose and do not have any religious-ritual basis. They are expressions of the instinct to adorn and beautify one's house, the primary unit in which the individual and the family spend their lives.

The walls of these types of houses generally provide the medium for washing with colour as well as sketching and painting a large variety of designs. These consist mostly of flowers, trees, creepers, birds, and animals. Then, there are the geometric designs. On the latter a general remark may be made here. The Dongrias reveal a preference for triangular designs – a design which is both colourful and impressive. It appears liberally on the scarf which they themselves weave on small looms. The Gadabas, on the other hand, are fond of squares and rectangles. These two groups rarely use circles or other complex geometrical patterns.

The colour of reddish earth provides the background for the walls which serve as the canvas. The clay paste is smeared and allowed to dry. The Santals tend to extend the frontiers of their imagination by drawing a cow eager to feed its calf; a peacock on a tree or elephants in the forest almost moving in a herd; swans gliding in water; elephants standing face to face with their trunks joined; and a baffling variety of trees, and other motifs. One does not notice any attempt of surrealistic presentation as in Saora pictograms. Here the attempt is at realism and depiction of a known reality. The houses of the Santals indeed look very colourful because instead of just patches of colour or paintings, their entire wall-faces are colour-washed.

The Santals use mostly coloured earth for painting the walls of their houses. They are very lucky in this regard. For in their local area, three colours which they prize for this purpose – white earth, red earth, and yellow earth – are generally available. People dig up and collect earth of these colours and bring them to their houses for giving a colour wash to the wall. The fourth primary colour which they use is black. Since no earth of this colour is available, they prepare it from indigenous materials. The wall-paintings of the other tribal groups are merely variations on Santal wall-paintings.

Considering the various facets of the creativity of the Orissan tribes in the field of ritual arts, one cannot fail to admire their sense of intricate design, their love of symmetry and harmonious form, their passionate feeling for colours, and their inherent impulse to decorate and adorn not only the human body, but also their houses and the general environment of the village. This only goes to prove that artistic creation is not necessarily a result of affluence and economic growth, for most of these tribal communities still live well below the poverty line.

D.H. KOPPAR

MAHARASHTRA

In the anthropological map of India, modern state political boundaries do not act as barriers in so far as the composition and distribution of one and the same tribal community in more than one state is concerned. For example, the Warli, Kukana, Dhodia, Dubla, and Koli are commonly found in both Gujarat and Maharashtra. They live in the same type of habitat in these regions. Their general level of culture and contextual background of art are the same.

Gujarat and Maharashtra along with Rajasthan form cognate cultural units in western India. Although, the tribal groups living in this region have many things in common, each has maintained its own cultural identity. The tribes in this region, as in others, live a hard and monotonous life. Indeed, theirs is a struggle for survival. Being food-gatherers originally, they have few material possessions. Living as they do in the fastness of the forests and the hills, they have imbibed from the soil a sturdy character and love for freedom. Although steeped in poverty and squalor, they have evolved a symbiotic relationship with their environment.

The quest of food takes most of their time and their entire social life revolves around rites and rituals, beliefs and superstitions, and ancestor worship. Yet, as the late Pandit Jawaharlal Nehru pointed out, they have something that we have lost and that is the spirit of song and dance and the capacity for enjoyment.

After all, what is there, one may ask, to inspire art in the hut of a tribal? What inspiration can their poverty, ignorance, and depression provide? What can one expect from a people who have lived, generation after generation, a life wherein they have to adjust themselves to the changing moods of nature, and experience a constant struggle for existence?

But like all human beings, the tribals find ways to express their creative impulses. Their religious ethos with its socio-religious rites and ceremonies of ancestor worship inspire artistic endeavour and are translated into dance or into sculpture and painting or decorative treatment of objects of everyday use. Every tribal material object has a story to tell, and enshrined in it is the pattern of the tribe's culture, its beliefs, its aspirations, and ideals.

Generally the materials used to fashion their art are wood, stone, and bamboo. The tools used by the tribal artist are the minimum and are indigenously made by him. The themes of tribal art are mainly religious and most of the objects have a ritual function. They are connected with various stages of life, memories of inter-tribal wars, the capture of cattle, the beginnings of agriculture indicating their transition from the food-gathering and hunting stage, their social and cultural life, urban society, birds and animals, and their environment. In Maharashtra, in 1981, the tribal population was fifty-seven lakhs which is nine per cent of the Indian tribal population. It is distributed in three zones: the Sahyadri, the Satpura, and the Gondwana. The Sahyadri zone includes the districts of Thane, Nasik, Pune, Ahmednagar, and Raigad and has been the home of such tribes as the Warlis, Kukana, Koli, and Thakar. Tribes such as the Bhils, Gavit, Dhanka, Pawara, Dubla, Pardhi, Tadavi, and Mawchi are found in the Satpura zone which encompassed Dhulia, Jalgaon, Amaravati, and Aurangabad districts. The districts of Gadachiroli, Chandrapur, Bhandara, Yavatmal, and Nanded form the Gondwana zone and the Gond, Kolam, Pardhan, and Andha tribes live here. Some tribes live in the fastness of the forests and the hill regions, while others live in the region of the plains.

Wall-paintings

Among the tribes of this region it is a common practice to draw designs on the walls. The theme of such drawings are mainly religious and inter-related with some of their important festivals. The Warlis and the Kukanas are good examples of living prehistory in Maharashtra. There is a close affinity between these groups. One has only to look at their rain gods carved in small black stone panels to be convinced. The anthropomorphic images of the rain gods bear a peculiar resemblance to the styles of images of Assyrian-Sumerian-Egyptian sculpture and add to the antiquity of their gods. Several years ago this writer happened to see these gods owned by a Warli family at Piprol, a village situated in a dense forest about two thousand feet above sea-level and about fourteen miles from Dharampur in south Gujarat. The fact that the culture of the Kukanas and the Warlis encompasses sun-worship, snake-worship, and worship of sacred stones and trees, together with such practices as tattooing, ear-piercing, and numerous other rites and beliefs, indicates that they are carriers of prehistoric traditions having contacts with the Mediterranean region.

The painting of the goddess of fertility was traditionally executed by the Warli women of Ganjad with rice flour paste on the mud walls of their huts at the time of a marriage ceremony in the family. This and other paintings are done with religious fervour during ceremonial rites.

1. Chandradev.
A mask of Chandradev or the moon god made of *pangara* wood. It is carved with the help of a tiny nail and hammer. This is a speciality of the Warli tribe. Coll: Tribal Research and Training Institute, Pune. Photo: Sunil Jadhav.

2

2. Palaghut Devi in a sacred circle.

Among the Warlis of western Maharashtra, at the time of a wedding the women of the family draw the sacred diagrams of Palaghut Devi with rice flour paste on the inner wall of their hut.

In recent years the men of the tribe have started practising this art which, formerly was, the exclusive domain of women. They execute the paintings on paper and unfettered by conventions they have produced very interesting portrayals of Warli life such as the sacred mountains, fields during monsoons, tribal group dance, and a spider's web. This painting, executed by the renowned Warli artist Jivya Soma depicts the sacred motif of the Palaghut Devi.
Photo: Chandu Mhatre.

3. Bhavani Mata.

A mask of the goddess Bhavani Mata.
Photo: courtesy Lady Wilson Museum, Dharampur, Gujarat.

3

4. Leather mask.
Coll: Tribal Research and
Training Institute, Pune.
Photo: Sunil Jadhav.

5. *Kodhal* mask.
This religious mask of the
Kolam tribe, used in the *Demsa*
dance. Every year, a new mask
is made and the old one
destroyed.
Coll: Tribal Research and
Training Institute, Pune.
Photo: Sunil Jadhav.

5

The process of drawing is interspersed with invocatory singing by a group of women and watched by others. Initially, they draw the *chaukat* (sacred square) which is ornamented with geometrical designs such as diamonds, triangles, and crosslines in alternating black and white resembling the movement of snakes. They make their own indigenous brush and the colour paste. The sun, the moon, the stars, and other gods are drawn around the goddess.

The technique of drawing the goddess herself is interesting. First an isosceles triangle is drawn on which another inverted isosceles triangle is placed and slanted vertical lines are drawn in the triangles. Then small legs, hands raised in benediction, and the head are symbolically indicated. A mystic aura surrounds the entire conception of the goddess and her implicit supernatural power. She emanates benevolent as well as malevolent qualities and therefore needs to be appeased by sacrifices and feasts.

No marriage can take place among the Warlis without first drawing the figure of Palaghut Devi on the wall of the central cell in their home. The bride and the bridegroom are made to sit below the wall-drawing on the ground to ensure a happy married life. In effect Palaghut Devi functions as the divine witness to the marriage, thus ensuring a happy married life for the prospective young couple. On the auspicious day when the marriage *pandal* (pavilion) is erected, the goddess is propitiated by the offering of a sacrificial hen which is killed on the lap of the bridegroom. In the painting the god Himaydev is depicted in the form of a cow.

The Panchavi or Pachhavi is another type of painting executed on the day of *Nag-Panchami* (July-August) when snakes, particularly cobras are worshipped. The painting is also made during the *Dussera* festival (October) and denotes the harvest season.

The Panchavi figure is drawn on the wall of the hut, with rice flour paste. Its square form contains three or more diminishing squares within it. Perhaps this represents a raised square platform. Occasionally, this platform takes the form of a circle. In any case it seems to be a stylized representation or symbol of the snake or sun. Above the square or circle, on either side is featured a tree with symmetrical branches. On top of the tree a peacock is shown. On the left side of the tree is depicted a snake holding a small mouse in its mouth and on the right another snake on its way towards the main totem in the centre. On the left-hand side of the panel the sun, the moon, and several scorpions are drawn. Some bullocks and men are shown in movement and on the right-hand side below a toddy tree with a group of people

Terracottas.
Made either as votive objects or toys, the terracottas display a very primitive power.

6

7

6. Votive animal.
The provision for wheels indicates that this figure served as an offering on fulfilment of a vow.
Coll: Tribal Research and Training Institute, Pune.
Photo: Sunil Jadhav.

7. Bhutyasur.
A forest deity, signalling the presence of evil spirits.
Coll: Tribal Research and Training Institute, Pune.
Photo: Sunil Jadhav.

Metal artefacts.

The use of metal is only a few centuries old. The tribals make their objects using the lost wax process.

8

9

8. Deities.
Two female deities seated in an enclosure. The execution is not evolved.
Coll: Tribal Research and Training Institute, Pune.
Photo: Sunil Jadhav.

9. Horse rider.
Although the technique is similar to that of Bastar, it is much cruder in execution.
Coll: Tribal Research and Training Institute, Pune.
Photo: Sunil Jadhav.

10. Metal containers.
Tobacco containers decorated with geometrical patterns that define, as well as are defined by the shape of the object.
Coll: Tribal Research and Training Institute, Pune.
Photo: Sunil Jadhav.

10

Wood carving.
Wood carving is popular among the tribals because of the easy availability of this material. Gods and goddesses, combs, masks, tobacco containers as well as ornaments are fashioned from this material.

11. Female deity.
The traditions of art in Maharashtra are closely related to those of Madhya Pradesh as both these areas are contiguous to one another. This figure exemplifies the qualities of strength and boldness associated with tribal art.
Coll: Tribal Research and Training Institute, Pune.
Photo: Sunil Jadhav.

11

some of whom are busy tapping toddy from the tree. A typical tribal hut with a standing couple and a child complete the entire drawing of the Panchavi.

On the *Nag-Panchami* day the tribals observe a fast, bathe, worship their domesticated animals such as bullocks, buffaloes, cows, and sheep and let them loose for grazing. When the animals return home in the evening, the tribals worship the goddess Panchavi drawn on the wall and celebrate the festival with a feast at night. Men, women, and children dance in the night to the accompaniment of the musical instrument *tarapu*. The totem symbol of the Panchavi is thus honoured and worshipped on that day.

Elsewhere, in other Panchavi drawings of the Warlis and the Kukanas the sun symbol serves as the central motif and all other figures converge towards it. During this festival the agricultural operations are in full swing and the people worship the sun for all the prosperity and happiness

12. *Musada.*
A wooden mask used during a dance to celebrate the fulfilment of a vow. Family deities are often depicted in these masks.
Coll: Tribal Research and Training Institute, Pune.
Photo: Sunil Jadhav.

12

it has bestowed on them. The entire painting suggests a vast movement of men and animals amidst a festive atmosphere.

The ceremonial drawings of the Kukanas and the Warlis use the same canvas—the wall of the house. The purpose of these drawings is to seek protection from animals, to increase fertility, and to avert diseases. The gods are called upon often to intervene in the simple but confused lives of the tribals and they are offered appeasement in order to help the tribals tide over the various crises that punctuate their lives.

The tribal artist pays attention to the minutest details in his painting and then dedicates it to the god or gods whom he wants to propitiate. Sometimes such paintings are the result of certain vows taken by a person in times of stress and strain caused by malevolent deities or malignant diseases. Such paintings thus have a votive significance.

These paintings are not devoted to a single theme but represent a combination of several concepts. Even though the depiction in their sacred paintings has been standardized to some extent, there is enough scope for the tribal artists to use their creative abilities. They are keen observers of nature and it provides them with a sense of form. The tribal artists see clear images in their vision before they actually begin their work. They experience flashes of insight through supernatural power and the work takes concrete shape in a state of frenzy. The tribal artist does not wrestle with techniques or forms: it is the content which determines the form. The paintings are imbued with rhythm, balance, and movement.

The Ganjad artist, who once painted with the same religious fervour, now paints on brown paper for commercial purposes. Without the magical evocation and tribal connotations, his art assumes a more stylized and stagnant expression. And yet, his paintings are not devoid of

13

14

13. Memorial pillar.
Such pillars are carved in memory of the dead and are erected in graveyards.
Coll: Tribal Research and Training Institute, Pune.
Photo: Sunil Jadhav.

14. *Devmundha*, marriage pillar.
Decorative pillars are carved by the bridegroom after his engagement.
Coll: Tribal Research and Training Institute, Pune.
Photo: Sunil Jadhav.

15. Basket.
Beautifully decorated with
birds and tassels, this basket is
used for the belongings of the
bride when she leaves for her
husband's home. The basket is
carried on the head and the
long tassels hang behind
covering the hair of the bearer.
Coll: Tribal Research and
Training Institute, Pune.
Photo: Sunil Jadhav.

15

merit, they throb with human and social themes and are secular in intent even when they portray religious symbols.

Masks

Another tribal art-form is the mask which serves as a disguise for the face. Often it is a grotesque representation of a face and is worn in dramas or dances. These masks portray forms of animals, birds, gods and goddesses, as well as demons and ghosts. They are made of clay, wood, bamboo, or papier-mâché.

Masks are very popular among the Kukanas and the Warlis of Gujarat and Maharashtra. They are used on ceremonial occasions when dramas are performed to the accompaniment of music and dance. During the festivals of *Holi* and *Divali* mask-shows are organized by itinerant tribal artists in different villages.

Masks are generally employed in dances and dramas presenting religious and mythological themes. The popular mask of Ravana, the imperishable villain of the great Indian epic, *Ramayana* is an arch-shaped framework made of bamboo strips and decorated with multi-coloured papers. Nine clay-head models with make-up in appropriate colours are affixed at the bottom of the arch.

The bison-horn mask and the *Kodhal* used by the Madia Gonds of Chandrapur district of Maharashtra are used on ceremonial occasions. The *Chandradev* mask is used in *Bhavada* performances in Maharashtra. Masks serve the purpose of tribal unity and stability and inculcate respect for tribal traditions and ancestors.

When making a mask, the tribal artist first decides on the size of the mask—generally larger than the human face—and then fills in details. Painting on the mask is done not as part of the enrichment of the sculpture, but as a means by which the spirit is infused into the mask and thus it comes to life. For example, the mask of Bhavani Mata used by the Warlis and the Kukanas of Maharashtra and Gujarat is painted in deep red to facilitate the entry of the spirit in the object.

Musical Instruments

The Kukanas, the Warlis, the Dhodias, and the Gonds make their own musical instruments from materials such as gourds, wood, and bamboo. Music and dance not only enliven their humdrum existence but serve also as repositories which have preserved their folklore. Their instruments are simple. The most popular is the *pavri* or *tarapu*. It is considered as the divine instrument of the Kukanas in both Maharashtra and Gujarat. The making of the *tarapu* is rooted in the idiom of tribal soil and bears the stamp of their artistic talent and creation. Made of gourd, it is used specially during religious ceremonies such as the worship of the Mahuli (mountain god). The melody of the *tarapu* is often used as accompaniment to dance.

The *ghangali* is a stringed instrument employed by the Kukanas, the Warlis, and the Dhodias. It is generally used while singing folk-songs. On special ceremonial occasions such as the Parjan—the periodic death anniversary ceremony of the Dhodias—the *Naika bhagat,* the priest of the Dhodias, plays it while directing the rites of the ceremony.

Madal is a majestic and sacred double-headed musical instrument of the Kukanas and the Warlis and it is prepared from a whole tree trunk and is fitted with animal skin. Its rhythmic beats guide the dancers in their intricate movements and foot-work.

Today, the tribal people are passing through a critical period of transition. The exposure to the rapidly changing new world is suffocating their creative impulses; the continuity and meaning attached to their art traditions are gradually ebbing away. The future of tribal art depends largely on the future of the tribal people. This means that the core of tribal life and the basic features of its culture have to be preserved because tribal art is rooted in tribal life. It is essential to determine what is enduring in tribal art through a systematic survey and a scientific evaluation of their art objects. Unless extensive documentation of the extant tribal art objects, their traditions, and multifarious forms, as also their tools and equipment is undertaken, the tribal component of the Indian heritage will be irretrievably lost. Ultimately, the future of Indian tribal art will lie in its ability to evolve, adjust, and adapt to the demands of the present.

GUJARAT

Chelio is a Rathwa tribal from the Baroda district of Gujarat. He wears a cadmium yellow turban with a green, blue, or red shirt and a short *lungi* (cloth tied to the waist). When he travels he wears a khaki dress like the one worn by beat-guards. He keeps a small knife and a flute with him always; they are his two constant companions.

Chelio lives a joyful life. He tills his field, climbs palm trees to tap palm juice, he swims or walks for miles along river banks, in the forests or in the mountains. He is not afraid of wild beasts, in fact, he talks of tigers as if they were his friends. He makes ropes from the bark of trees, fashions spoons out of wood, and containers out of bamboo. He makes his own flute, and plays on it for hours. He knows exactly which bamboo, of which colour, how thick and long, and of what season, would make the best flute. He creates flutes which range from twenty centimetres to one hundred centimetres in length. Sometimes he carves figures on the flute with his knife. At other times he paints horses, tigers, kings, and gods on the walls of his hut for hours without a break. Like Chelio, his sister and wife possess an instinctive feeling for the environment—they adorn themselves with jewellery made from glass beads, seeds, and shells. In several tribes, women help in many tasks such as fishing.

Festivals play a pivotal role in the life of the tribals. They provide occasions for dressing-up in finery and dancing with abandon. Wherever he may be, the tribal does not forget the spring festival, *Holi,* when he decorates his body with paint and dances with his friends for days on end. Thus, in the tribal communities, art and life dovetail into one continuous process.

From birth, the creative impulse of the tribal finds expression in his everyday activities. As a child he roams about in natural surroundings, creating different forms from flowers, leaves, twigs and bamboo, from fruits, feathers, gourds, and grass. Clay, the ever-present material is marvellous to mould and shape. The tribal develops extraordinary skills as he learns to make the best use of the limited resources available to him. The tribals build their houses by themselves, occasionally with the help of their neighbours. These homes are made of local materials. Their sense of air, weather, and mother earth is very sharp; they know exactly where, how, and when to build. The house is sanctified by rituals and ceremonies, some of which are repeated periodically. For the house is not only a shelter for the living members of the family, but also an integral part of themselves, their ancestors, and their gods. Each element in the house is therefore, of great value. Among the Bhil Garasia tribe, for example, the house is built around a huge jar approximately eight metres high and three metres in diameter. Thus the storage jar can never be taken out of the house. These are veritable sculptured beings living among the inmates of the house.

Wall-paintings

Just as they adorn their bodies, the tribals decorate their homes and belongings with designs. On the walls of their homes they paint patterns with a broom or brushes made of *babul* twigs. The designs among the Rathwa tribals tend to be geometrical, while in the other communities animals and human figures are depicted. The function of these paintings is primarily decorative, though often it can be religious in character, as when there is a wedding in the family. At times, as in the case of Pithora paintings, the painting is made to avoid the god's wrath. Rites of appeasement play a prominent role in tribal life and several rituals serve as votive functions: they are performed in fulfilment of vows undertaken to avert calamities and bring about a sense of well-being.

Once a year the Chaudhari tribals celebrate their ancestors' day. They feed the ancestors by placing food as an offering on the roof of their homes. They then feed the hut and the storage jars, their tools and agricultural implements, and their livestock. They feed the house by painting certain motifs on the walls and the process is referred to as *ghar jamadyu* (the home has been offered a feast). For painting on the walls the tribal woman takes some *jowar* (millet) flour, mixes it with buttermilk, fills her mouth with it, and then sprays it on the wall creating a negative palm or footprint where she has placed her hand or foot. As against this negative print, she also makes positive prints by applying liquid colour on her palms or feet and imprinting them on the walls.

The Rathwa tribals attach a deep significance to Pithora, their tribal god. According to them Pithora Baba has been living in their homes from time immemorial. The painting is done on the hut walls for different reasons, for the appeasement of the deity whose wrath may be causing difficulties or for thanksgiving in times of prosperity. The Pithora painting is executed by a

1. A horse.
An exaggerated and imaginative rendering of a horse.
Photo: courtesy Haku Shah.

2. Tribal woman with silver ornaments.
The tribals purchase silver jewellery from village craftsmen. Such interactions between the tribal and village communities have existed for centuries often blurring the distinctions that prevail between the tribal and the folk traditions.
Photo: courtesy and copyright Jyoti Bhatt.

3. Festival decorations.
During *Holi,* boys decorate their bodies with painted dots or circles. They don feathers or bamboo baskets as headgear and dance, for days and days celebrating *Holi.* The men play on flutes with designs that they have etched on them. The women play the cymbals.
Photo: courtesy Haku Shah.

4. Masked performer.
Festivals include dance performances with masks and colourful costumes.
Photo: courtesy Haku Shah.

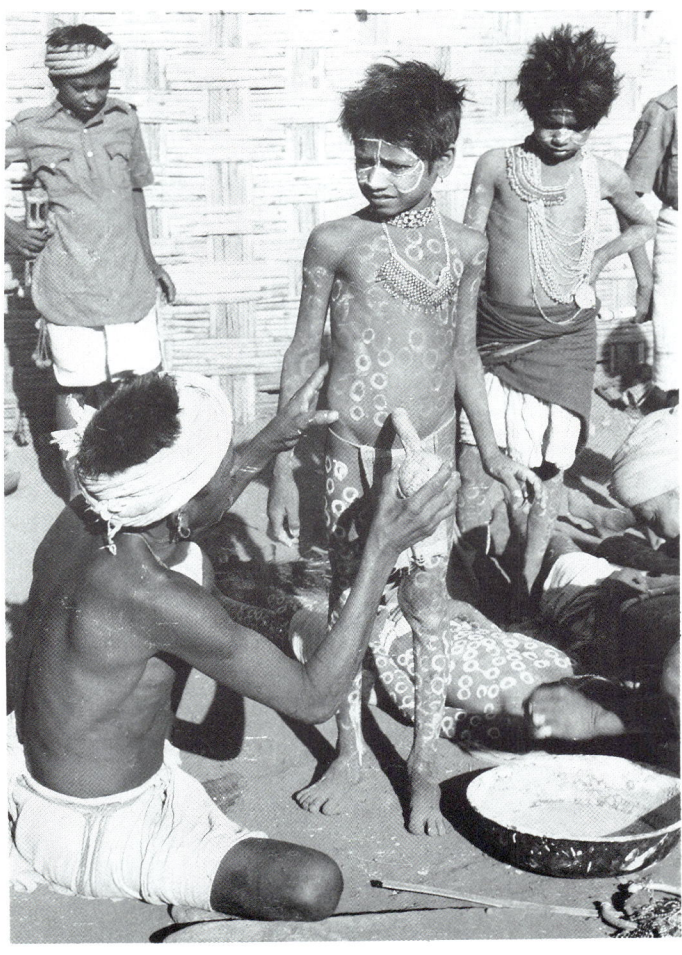

Wall decorations.

The Rathwa tribals adorn their huts with painted patterns which cover the entire wall surface including the pillars. The design is conceived in vertical panels with broad horizontal bands alternating with a series of narrow ones. Within each band a simple geometrical motif like a triangle, a circle or a semicircle is featured and is replicated throughout the panel. Despite its simplicity the painting is impressive because of its inherent sense of overall design and continuity. The artistry is evident in the variations that are effected while laying out the bands and the manner in which the motifs are treated in size as also in mass— sometimes as solids, at other times as voids.

5. Paintings on a Rathwa hut.
The design is executed in white on dull yellowish brown cowdung smeared walls. The contrast is striking as well as appealing. Occasionally the design is conceived with sytlized motifs of flowers and plants. Among many tribal communities the task of decorating the hut is assigned to the women in the family.
Photo: courtesy and copyright Jyoti Bhatt.

group of painters called Lakharas who work together as a team. The motif of a horse is drawn partly by hand and partly by means of a block. The technique employed in one such case was as follows : Lakhara Bhuro placed the block firmly on the wall in position with the front portion of the horse's torso held slightly upwards and the rear part a little lower. Then he pressed the thumb of his left hand in the centre of the block pushing it against the wall with the weight of the whole hand. He clasped the knife firmly in his other hand and moved its sharp edge around the block. He drew the upper part of the two hind legs first and then completed the front legs. Here he used a little pressure with his index finger, to twist the line at an angle. He then drew the lower portion of the hind legs in the same manner. Using his index finger again, he pressed

6. New motifs in wall-paintings.
As the tribals become exposed to the outside world, elements of that world are introduced in their wall-paintings. In this panel a truck is incorporated – somewhat capriciously – in the traditional design. The inclusion of such motifs will gradually lead to alterations and modifications in the inherited traditional forms.
Photo: courtesy and copyright Jyoti Bhatt.

7. Chaudhari tribal woman feeding the house.
To the tribals their home is but an extension of themselves. For instance among the Chaudhari tribes the ceremonies of ancestor worship include painting the walls of the house. This activity is referred to as *ghar jamadyu* (offering a feast to the house).

The painting is done by taking *jowar* (millet) flour, mixing it in buttermilk, and then a woman from the family fills her mouth with this liquid and sprays it on the wall where she has placed her palm or foot. The result is a negative print. This is the opposite of a positive print which they make by dipping their palms or feet in coloured or white liquid and making imprints on the walls.
Photo: courtesy and copyright Jyoti Bhatt.

8. Spray painted auspicious objects in a Chaudhari home.
In addition to negative palm and footprints, they also create negative prints of kitchen knives and farm implements.
Photo: courtesy and copyright Jyoti Bhatt.

6

7

8

down on the knife to incise the lower part of the neck in an arc working from the top of the neck. He held the knife in such a manner that with a slight pressure of his forefinger he could execute another arc above. Next he delineated the horse's mane over the neck. Even though it is difficult, an experienced hand can make firm drawings by means of a knife. The knife incisions are marked by lines of brownish ochre on white clay priming. The painter works only with the pointed edge of the knife and his lines are sure, requiring no erasures.

In the meanwhile other Lakharas painted the horses in orange. The tigers had already been drawn. Lakhara Tetiya started working on the elephant, painting it blue. A circular space within the elephant's body was kept blank, while the rest of it had been filled in with colour. Tetiya then drew a fan-like figure within the blank space called *kaya dev*. Two persons, one of whom was Raja Bhoj, was shown sitting on a *howdah* on the elephant's back, with a *mahout* sitting in front of them. The *mahout* and the elephant were drawn in profile but the elephant had two eyes. To the right of the elephant, a farmer, called Halapati Raja, the lord of the plough, was shown with two bulls. Some Lakharas drew, while others filled in the colours. Towards the top of the wall, the figure of Hudol was completed in silver paint. The remaining picture space was then filled up with motifs representing things that the tribals encounter in their everyday life. So the painting depicted Pithora and his wife accompanied by kings and ancestors as well as a retinue of horses and elephants. In addition to these were scenes from myths and legends. Then the picture space was covered with depictions of tigers, serpents, dogs, deer, monkeys, camels, bulls, cows, trees, storage jars, scorpions, cars, trains, and aeroplanes. Occasionally images from dreams and fantasy line this mural painting.

On such occasions in the evening after the professional drummers arrive the *badvo* priest, an aged man with long hair, sits next to the wall on which the painting of Pithora Baba has been executed. The head of the household, arrives with a lamp in his hand and goes towards the painting. He holds the lamp in his left hand and gently moves his right palm over the flame towards the painting as a token of offering and does the same towards the *badvo*. Then commences the ritual of identification of the figures in the painting. The *badvo* sits in silence for a while, and gradually enters into a trance; his head sways in a circular movement and he starts muttering. One of the lakharas holds a lamp near the painting. The *badvo* seizes a sword in his left hand, and with his right hand points at figures in the painting one by one and recounts stories from the mythological episodes that are featured there.

9, 10. Pithora wall-paintings.
Various tribal communities of Gujarat like the Rathwas, the Shilalas, and the Naikus, paint Pithora Baba on their hut walls. The painting is votive in nature and is offered as fulfilment of vows taken for the supplication of the deity in times of stress and difficulty. The painting is done by a group of painters called Lakharas. At first the horse is delineated and painted. Thereafter are painted Pithora, his consort, and other figures like Raja Bhoj seated on the elephant and the lord of the plough represented by a farmer ploughing with a pair of bullocks. Scenes from their myths and objects that they encounter in their day to day existence are also included as subjects in the painting. The picture space is filled with representations of animals such as tigers, camels, and monkeys, as well as serpents, peacocks, and scorpions.
Fig. 9: photo courtesy and copyright Jyoti Bhatt.
Fig. 10: photo courtesy Haku Shah.

9

Terracotta figures.
Terracotta figures play an important role in tribal cultures. Although they may be used as toys, more often than not they are intended as votive offerings to various deities. Interestingly, these figurines are not made by the tribals themselves but by the village potters – often women. The village potters are familiar with the iconographic requirements of the tribals and are able to produce exactly what they need. The techniques employed in creating some of these images – such as pinching, pressing, and slitting – show an unbroken continuity from the time of the Indus Valley Civilization which flourished five thousand years ago.

11

11. A horse rider.
Tribal shamans make this type of figure for curing diseases.
Photo: courtesy Haku Shah.

94

He also correlates the situations painted there to the everyday experience of the tribal. Thus he moves from one plane to another from the sacred to the profane. The *badvo* comes out of his trance and rushes outside and it is at this time that the groups of men, women, and children who have come from different villages in the area are seen dancing outside. There is a festive atmosphere in the village. Finally, with the smear of blood of the sacrificial goat, the painting of the Pithora Baba is complete.

In this ritual, all the art-forms intertwine into one, that of painting, music, dance, and drama. The trance experience, the feasting, and celebrating impart to the ritual a totality of form which is vibrant and intense. In tribal rituals works of art are the indispensable and focal means of communication with the Supernatural, with man's experience of the Real. The Real is sensed in the waking experience. It may be adumbrated in dreams; it is known in trance. Trance, dream, and waking experiences are actual, though vary in kind and degree, and lie in different, but unconnected planes. Tribal art gives them form. The ritual of the Pithora is common also among other tribal groups such as the Bhilala and the Naika.

Terracottas

Terracottas, made of mother earth have always presented a great wealth of living art-forms in India from early times—from the Harappan cities of the third millennium BC till today. Amazingly, the technique employed thousands of years ago prevails even today in places in the Surat district where women potters in the villages make the terracotta figurines for the

12. Two witches on a two-headed horse.
Tribal shamans make such images from clay obtained from anthills.
Photo: courtesy Haku Shah.

12

13. A tribal shrine in a forest.
Tribals offer animal and bird sacrifices to appease their capricious deities. Their rituals include the offering of grains as well as terracotta figures as thanksgiving for boons received or to ward off future calamities.
Photo: courtesy and copyright Jyoti Bhatt.

14. Offerings to a terracotta horse.
Among the Bhil Garasias the terracotta horse figure becomes the recipient of offerings of grain after the crop is harvested.
Photo: courtesy Haku Shah.

15. A forest shrine.
Underneath a tree in a forest grove is a tribal deity. Placed around it are a dome and votive terracotta offerings of a tiger and a horse.
Photo: courtesy and copyright Jyoti Bhatt.

13

14

15

tribals to use in their rituals. While creating the terracotta horse the potter believes that it is being infused with *jiva* (soul). And for the tribal too, this terracotta forms a link between him and his god : it is not an inanimate object.

When the Bhil Garasia tribal comes to buy a terracotta elephant or a horse, the ritual of buying begins. A lamp is lit, and offered to the figure, *prasad* (offering) of coconut is served to it and to all who are there and only then is that figure lifted. At this time, the potter bids farewell to the terracotta figure he had created. With love and care he gently places the figure on the tribal's head or shoulder, and the proud owner carries it with great devotion, for, even a small crack in the terracotta figure will render it inauspicious. From the potter's home, the tribal often walks miles carrying the figure to god Tubraj's sanctuary. These sacred abodes are always in remote areas, either high up in the mountains or near a group of boulders in a forest grove, in a thicket or near a stream or river—always at a mystic spot. The sanctuary is guarded by the *chokidar* (watchman) and *nakedar* (guard) at the corners. Some minor deities have to be propitiated before one approaches the god Tubraj. The tribals believe that the tigers are the watch-dogs of the gods, as they are often found in the vicinity of these areas.

At such sanctuaries thousands of terracottas can be seen. Each year they are offered. And as the winds, the sun, and the rain destroy some, their place is taken by new ones. Sundays and Tuesdays are considered special days when terracottas are offered at large sanctuaries. Often the same god, has an abode in the village and this shrine is known as *utaro* (a place to rest). If the tribal is unable to go to the distant sanctuary, he can offer objects to his deity at the *utaro*. Village deities like Kaka Balia (god of small pox) and Kansari Devi (goddess of agriculture) have their abodes in different villages.

Various tribal groups such as the Chaudharis, the Gamits, the Dublas, the Dhankas, and the Vasawas offer terracotta objects to their gods and goddesses in propitiation and supplication for the well-being of an individual or a village, for protection against harassment by evil spirits; for guarding against ill health or as a part of the disease-curing ritual, or for the recovery of lost property. Terracotta figures are offered also to ancestors in ceremonies for installing the spirits of the dead.

These terracottas are found sometimes in twos or threes outside a hut, under a tree, or in a field, at other times in a cluster of thousands in a large secluded area or in a procession under a grove of trees. Generally, these terracotta figures are offered by individuals or families, but occasionally the inhabitants of the village get together as a community and make such offerings.

16. Votive terracottas.
Thousands of terracotta figurines are offered every year and lie untended. Over a period of time the elements take their toll and the figurines disintegrate only to be replaced with new ones. Several tribes in Gujarat like the Bhil Garasias, Bhils, Chaudharis, Rathwas, Dublas, and the Vasawas offer terracotta horses for wish-fulfilment and in propitiation for their future well-being.
Photo: courtesy and copyright Jyoti Bhatt.

17, 18. Bhil Garasia shrine.
In the Bhil Garasia community there is a custom whereby they place terracotta plaques with representations of gods and goddesses (including some Hindu divinities) as offerings in the shrine. To make place for the new offerings the old ones are removed and placed outside the shrine or discarded in a heap. Photos: courtesy and copyright Jyoti Bhatt.

The journey to the sacred sanctuary is often long and arduous. The tribals have to camp at night at some spot. Through the long dark hours of the night, beneath the vast starlit sky, to the vibrant accompaniment of the *dev dovdi* (god's guard) and the incessant chanting of the priests in a trance, the tribals dance and sing in unison, invoking the presence of the gods and goddesses. After this, still singing and dancing, they proceed towards the sacred sanctuary where a number of people participate in the sacrificial ritual. Together with the offering of the terracotta figure, the tribal makes offerings of food, wine, rice, coins, flags, flowers, coconuts, lamps, incense, and the sacrificial chicken or the goat. When the terracotta is stained with the blood of the sacrificial animal, it becomes a worthy offering.

The tribals claim that their combined fervour makes the terracotta come alive and their deity would accept it with affection. Dancing and feasting follows this ritual. Later the priest installs a flag on the top of a tree and scatters rice on the people below who collect it and put it in a clay storage jar. With the blessings of the god, the tribals believe that their crops will be bountiful. These terracotta forms—large or small — represent the mind, heart, and the spirit of both the potter who made the object, and the tribal who used it in a sacred ritual. They also embody an attitude that is down to earth, respectful of the material, technique, and the act of creativity that shaped the clay into a form.

Wooden Figures

For the tribals, the art-form evolves naturally from their way of life which is hard and full of unpredictable situations. In Gujarat, the Chaudharis, the Gamits, and the Vasawas erect and worship wooden crocodile gods to extricate themselves from difficulties. A woman belonging to the Chaudhari tribe, who did not have a son vowed that she would install a crocodile god and worship it if she gave birth to a son. When a son was born to her, true to her vow, she installed a crocodile god. This happened forty-five years ago. Her son still lives in the village. Bhagat Ratadra Jeltria, the carver of the crocodile image in Amba village (near Sangadh), recounted, "This crocodile was installed because the cattle were dying, there was no milk and all the children were in danger of perishing. Tigers were attacking the cattle and the crops were wilting. The tribal people offered worship to all the gods, and I brought them together in this wood—in this powerful wooden crocodile that I carved. That was ten years ago. The god (crocodile) proved good and true : the calamity was averted. Now, they worship the crocodile all the twelve months of the year." Wooden crocodiles are also erected to save crops from getting adversely affected or to guard cattle from disease and death.

19. The divine crocodile.
Made of wood, this god is supposed to be powerful and is worshipped by a person desiring a male offspring or by people hoping to avert a calamity like famine or persistent attacks by wild beasts. Photo: courtesy and copyright Jyoti Bhatt.

20. Funerary dome.
Mortuary rites and ancestor worship are an integral part of tribal culture. In the Chaudhari tribe when a person dies a painting signifying the spirit of the departed person is executed by the priest in *sindur* and oil on a stone tablet referred to as *khatru*. The relatives adorn the figure with silver ornaments, perform the feeding ritual, carry the tablet in a procession, dancing and singing to the grave site. The painted figure is placed in a terracotta funerary domed object called *ghumat*. Such domes usually are clustered under a large tree. Photo: courtesy and copyright Jyoti Bhatt.

19

Funerary Memorials

Nandaria Devalia Vasava died in June 1972. Khataria Pukhia of Tokarva village, a close relative of Nandaria, participated in the ceremony of installing a *khambha* (memorial pillar). He said that during the rainy season. While brewing wine in the marshland near Kataskuva village Nandaria, was accosted by Pandu, the policeman. Frightened, Nandaria left the pot and ran away, and hung himself with a rope from a tree lest his father or mother scold him; thus he ended his life. Nandaria was deaf and dumb and was loved by all the villagers. Because he did not die a natural death it was commonly believed that his spirit would wander aimlessly, unless it was given a place to rest in the form of a memorial pillar. Thus, a pillar with the figure of a man carved on it was ordered. On the day of the installation, the *khambha* was draped in a *dhoti,* put in a cart and to the accompaniment of singing and music it was escorted to the place where it was to be erected. Uttam, a carpenter, took the *khambha* and began to bore a hole in it for the *jiva.* The priest uttered some words, and from a small heap of rice placed nearby he threw a few grains of rice, some water, and some liquor into a pit. The priest offered twenty paise, others made similar offerings. The *khambha* with a hole bored in the right side of the breast for the *jiva* to rest in, was firmly inserted into the pit facing east. In a trance, the priest put the *jiva* into the hole of the *khambha* and the carpenter covered the hole with a wooden piece thereby sealing the soul into the pillar.

Among the Chaudhari tribals, when a person dies, a painting signifying the spirit of the departed person is done by the priest in the presence of all assembled. The priest executes the painting with *sindur* (vermilion) and oil. The relatives adorn this painted effigy with clothing and ornaments and offer food. The stone tablets, called *khatru,* are then placed in a basket which is carried on the head by a relative to the grave site. The other relatives join him in a procession. They sing and dance as they go along and thus the spirit of the dead also dances and begins an unending pilgrimage to the mystic grave.

At the grave site, the painted stone is placed in a new terracotta funerary house called *ghumat* (dome) that has been specially made for the spirit to dwell in. The ceremony concludes with feasting. The spirit of the ancestor is then invoked and offerings made to it. The descendants of the dead person observe these rituals for a minimum of twelve years. During that period, whenever a male member of the family passes the *khatru* he offers salutations to it and often presents a lighted *bidi* (native cigaratte) to it in a symbolic gesture of sharing and camaraderie.

Such funerary clay houses are usually clustered under a large grove of trees. The process of accretion and disintegration of these terracotta objects in the grave is continuous and within it reposes the heritage of the tribals.

The tribals in Gujarat comprise fourteen per cent of the total population. There are twenty-eight tribes, many of them spread into neighbouring Maharashtra, Rajasthan, and Madhya Pradesh. Tribal art celebrates "the Man". From morning till night, from birth to death, and even after, they celebrate; every act is dealt with physical, mental, and spiritual power. Life is lived in knowing the known and the unknown, in the process he creates innumerable works of art. Their socio-economic life, customs, fairs, and festivals play a vital role in determining their art-forms. Inspired by the environment, the tribal creates forms from materials that exist around him. Out of two leaves, Chaudhari tribals make *tada* and *tadi* (bridegroom and bride) as toys for children. Interestingly, the tribal knows instinctively the minimum and maximum usage of a material, for example, they have found innumerable uses for the humble gourd; they make from it spoons, bowls, pots, as well as musical instruments.

Tribal art cannot be studied as a separate expression such as painting or sculpture. It has religious inspiration and it is enacted through music, dance, pantomimes, and trance. The art object is an essential part of this ritual. It is anonymous, created by individuals or a group. Its very essence is that it is ephemeral.

M.K. PAL

MADHYA
PRADESH

The arts and crafts of the tribals of Madhya Pradesh embody the creative imagination of the tribal craftsmen and craftswomen. They consist of objects fashioned with primitive artistic skills and tools, and they are utilitarian, decorative or ritualistic in nature. Originally, these objects served the needs of the common people in or around the centres of production, but nowadays they also satisfy the aesthetic taste of sophisticated people. These examples not only reflect the age-old ways of production of the tribals, their own designs, colour schemes, as well as individual shapes and patterns, but also represent unique artefacts impregnated with silent and subtle values.

The tribal crafts of Madhya Pradesh can be separated into three broad groups. The first comprises items that have utilitarian value and includes textiles, baskets, vessels for keeping domestic articles, oil containers, water pots, clay lamps, measuring bowls, stools for sitting, fishing traps, smoking pipes, tobacco cases, footwear, musical instruments, arrows for hunting, and weapons. The second group consists of decorative objects such as jewellery and ornaments, while the third and last group encompasses magico-religious objects mainly representing figures of deities which the tribals worship. It is important to note here that often non-tribal craftsmen produce a number of objects for the consumption of the tribal communities. These craft examples can, nevertheless, be termed as tribal art because they are basically tribal in their form, and their style of execution.

Utilitarian Objects

Textiles

The tribals employ a variety of textiles, using them for making cotton coats, skirts, saris, *chadars* (sheets), loincloths, blouses, veils, sleeveless jackets, bags, and caps. The Parjas of Bastar use the cotton coat and it is generally hand-woven and hand-coloured. They use the cotton cloth specially during ceremonial dances. The cotton skirt that they use is coloured dark orange. The Maria and Muria women of Narayanpur, Bastar, use an interesting variety of the sari; the surface of the cloth is mixed white and violet having the weft in white and the warp violet. They also prefer the *chadar* which is a coarse and loom-woven cloth. Among the Abujhmars of Bastar and the Bhils of Jhabua, the *angachi* (loincloth) is very popular. The Oraons of Raigarh and the Gonds of Chhindwara use a sleeveless jacket made of black and red cloth and sometimes printed in chocolate colour. The Bhil women of Jhabua drape the *orni* (veil) dyed in black and printed in red, yellow, and white. The Bhils of Mandugarh wear caps made of mill-made cloth. The Gonds of Chhindwara carry a purse made of cotton threads. The Korkus of Betul use a bag made of net for keeping money.

Baskets

Baskets made of bamboo and leaf are used for carrying and storing grains, and also for keeping the fish after the catch. They are found among the Bhils of Jhabua, the Korkus of Nimar as well as Raigarh, the Abujhmars of Bastar, and the Gonds of Chhindwara.

Vessels

Among the vessels used for domestic purposes special mention may be made of vessels made of gourd. The Marias and Murias of Bastar use them for keeping liquid substances. These vessels are of several shapes the most popular being a rounded form with a short neck. Sometimes stone bowls are also used for keeping domestic articles.

The Korkus of Betul and the Oraons of Raigarh use oil containers locally known as *dutua* or *chuka*. These are usually made on the wheel by the *kumbhars* (local potters). The water pots are generally made of clay and turned on the wheel in different shapes. The Kukshis and the Naikdas of Dhar are the main consumers of these pots.

The measuring bowls made of bamboo strips or wood are cylindrical with closed bottoms. The Marias of Bastar and the Gonds of Chhindwara are the main users of these bowls.

Stools

The *khatauli* (stools) are generally made of wood and fibre ropes. Firstly, the frame is made of wood having vertical stands at four corners, and then the top is woven with fibre ropes. The Murias, the Marias, and the Abujhmars of the Bastar region are known to be the main users of these stools.

Fishing Traps

The *kumna* (fishing traps) made of bamboo are used by many tribal communities of Madhya Pradesh specially the Baigas of Mandla. These traps are set in flowing water in a standing position to catch fish.

1. Mother.
The unpolished figure emphasizes the grain of the wood.
Coll: National Museum, New Delhi.
Photo: courtesy National Museum, New Delhi.

Wooden figures.

They appear to be secular in intent and inspired from relief carvings that occur on memorial pillars. Such figures are mostly of recent origin having a purely decorative function. In style as well as technique, they differ from wooden figures produced in the first half of the twentieth century. They are unpolished and the grain of the wood is taken into account while carving. This style of carving is typical of the Muria tribe of Bastar.

Smoking Pipes and Tobacco Cases

The tribals especially the Korkus of Betul and Nimar, the Gonds of Chhindwara, the Marias and Murias of Bastar, and the Korkus and Oraons of Raigarh use smoking pipes and tobacco cases generally made of clay and wood. The tobacco cases are egg-shaped, flat, circular or conical. These are also made of brass by the *cire perdue* process.

Hunting Implements and Weapons

Arrows of different sizes and types made of iron and bamboo are employed for killing snakes, hunting birds, and animals. These arrows are used by the Marias, the Murias, and the Dorlas of Bastar, the Bhils of Indore, the Korkus of Raigarh, the Naikras of Dhar, and the Gonds of Chhindwara. A special type of harpoon arrow is used by the Dorlas of Bastar for fishing.

The weapons used in warfare mainly consist of *dhal* (shields), *talwar* (swords), and *farsa* (axes). The shield and the sword are used chiefly by the Gond *Jagirdars* of Bilaspur, while the axe is used by other tribal communities like the Marias and Murias of Jagdalpur in Bastar, and the Bhils of Jhabua.

Footwear

Of the footwear used by the tribal people of Madhya Pradesh special mention may be made of the leather shoes decorated with gold or silver thread embroidery work. This is mainly used by the Bhilalas and the Kukshis of Dhar during marriage ceremonies.

Clay Lamps

The clay lamps turned on the wheel by local potters are generally conical, circular, and concave and used everyday by most of the tribal communities of Madhya Pradesh.

2. Wooden female figure.
Carved in a simplistic manner this figure from Bastar shows abbreviated treatment and little modelling.
Coll: National Museum, New Delhi.
Photo: courtesy National Museum, New Delhi.

3. Mother and child.
This seated figure holding a child in her lap is carved in fair detail delineating ornaments and hair-style.
Coll: National Museum, New Delhi.
Photo: courtesy National Museum, New Delhi.

2

3

105

Musical Instruments

The tribal people of Madhya Pradesh are very fond of music. They sing songs and dance on religious and ceremonial occasions to the accompaniment of different musical instruments such as wooden, brass, and iron cymbals, drums, metal bells, brass or bamboo flutes, horns made of brass or buffalo horn, and violins and other stringed instruments locally known as *tambura, ektara,* and *chikara* made from gourd-shell, bamboo, wood, skin, and wires. Another notable variety of musical instruments is the *nagara* played with sticks during a dance.

Decorative Objects

The decorative objects used by the tribal people of Madhya Pradesh mainly consist of a variety of jewellery and ornaments such as bangles, necklaces, finger-rings, ear-rings, anklets and armlets, forehead ornaments, ankle-bells, filets, hairpins and combs, necklets, pendants, neck-bands, ear-plugs, wristlets, amulets, headgears, and bison-horn head-dresses. They are made of silver, wood, brass, glass, imitation silver, lac or china clay, copper, bell-metal, bamboo, grass, and palm-leaf.

The bangles, usually made of silver, brass, copper, and lac are used by many tribal communities. Of the bangles, the silver ones are interesting because of their novel designs. Some of the silver bangles consist of several pieces of conical motifs which are strung on a red cotton string.

The different types of necklaces are made of copper, silver, glass beads, lac, and grass, and are very popular among the tribal people. The necklaces are simple, and are composed of glass beads strung together, while the copper and silver necklaces are commonly made by the lost wax process.

4. Marriage pole.
Carved and painted, this hollow pole is shaped like a man standing with raised hands. Photo: courtesy B. N. Aryan.

5. Wooden memorial pillar from Bastar.
The Murias erect such pillars on the roadside leading to their settlements. These pillars commemorate the death of an elder or an eminent person of that tribe. Carved in high relief on all four sides the pillar depicts scenes from everyday life.
Coll: National Museum, New Delhi.
Photo: courtesy National Museum, New Delhi.

6. Ceremonial dolls.
These standing figures – a male and a female – belong to the collection compiled by Verrier Elwin in the 1940s. Apparently, they were used for the Muria tribe dance performances. The style and treatment of the figures strikes as being rather curious and not in keeping with what is generally encountered in that region.
Coll: National Museum, New Delhi.
Photo : courtesy National Museum, New Delhi.

6

7. Carved doors.
Door shutters divided into square panels decorated in low relief with human, animal, and floral motifs. These designs are similar to those that occur on memorial pillars.
Coll: Dr Siddharth and Yashodhara-raje Bhansali.
Photo: Dr Siddharth Bhansali.

Finger-rings made of silver and brass are sometimes decorated with embossed designs. They are commonly used by most of the tribal people. The ear-rings made of silver and brass are also equally popular among the tribals.

The tribals also wear anklets and armlets. The anklets and armlets made of brass, bell-metal, and silver are manufactured by the lost wax process. The *ghunghru* (ankle-bells) usually made of brass by the *cire perdue* process consist of small bells which are tied in a row to a cotton string or a leather piece. These are used by many tribal communities of Madhya Pradesh.

Of the forehead ornaments made of silver, the semicircular tiara-type is the most popular particularly among the Korku women of Nimar. It is composed of several small bells attached in a row.

Filets made of brass sheets decorated with raised designs are generally used by the tribals as head decoration during dance performances. Hair ornaments such as the hairpins and combs are very common. The hairpins are made of an alloy and decorated with cowrie-shells, while the combs are made of wood, bamboo, brass or German-silver. Both the types are very popular among the tribals.

Necklets, pendants, and the neckbands appear to be a favoured form of ornamentation. The necklets are usually made of German-silver and brass by the *cire perdue* process, while the pendants and neckbands are composed of cylindrical glass beads. The necklets are circular and decorated with incised lines in spiral form.

Writstlets, made of brass and an alloy of tin and zinc, and ear-plugs made of wood, lac, and palm-leaf are very popular as ornaments.

Among other ornaments used by the tribals of Madhya Pradesh mention may be made of the amulets, headgears, and the bison-horn head-dresses which are not only popular, but also bear primitive characteristics in their style and form. The *sing-topi* (bison-horn head-dress) is made of cloth, wood, and peacock feathers, while the different headgears are made of bamboo strips and paper. Both types are used during dance performances.

8. Comb.
Wooden comb with an intricate pattern depicting a human figure in the centre of an archway with two birds perched atop.
Coll: National Museum, New Delhi.
Photo: courtesy National Museum, New Delhi.

9. Mask of a diseased person.
As in the north-east, so also in Madhya Pradesh, masks representing diseased persons were used to scare away evil spirits. This mask represents a man with discoloured skin and boils. Animal hair is attached to the scalp and the eyebrows.
Coll: National Museum, New Delhi.
Photo: courtesy National Museum, New Delhi.

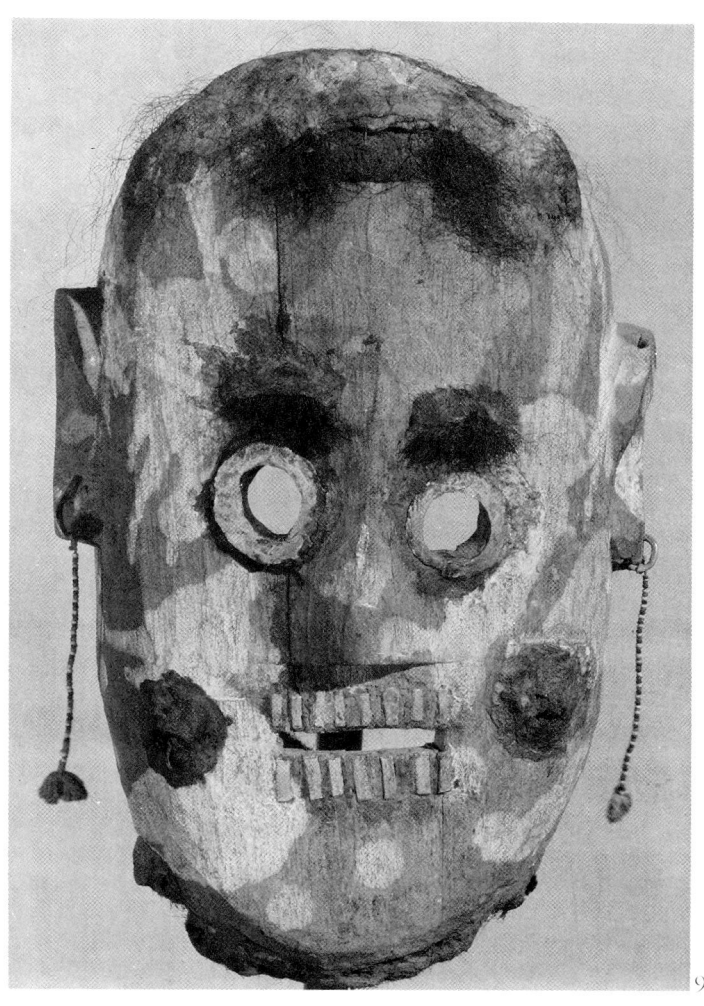

8

9

10

10. Terracotta votive elephant.
The elephant is carrying an auspicious pot as thanksgiving on the fulfilment of a vow. Such terracottas are placed in sacred sanctuaries outside tribal settlements. Painted in black and white the elephant is rendered in basic shapes of round, oval, and square as it is put together from different pots. It is composed of a pot with an elaborate lid placed on another pot which rests on the elephant's back shaped to receive it and hold it in place.
Coll: National Museum, New Delhi.
Photo: courtesy National Museum, New Delhi.

11. *Chiria chun-mun* roof-tiles.
Roof-tiles shaped in the form of birds are used in the areas bordering Bihar and Madhya Pradesh. Not only do they serve the function of decoration but also attract real birds. They are known as *chiria chun-mun*.
Photo: courtesy and copyright Jyoti Bhatt.

12. A votive animal.
Often terracottas on wheels have been interpreted as toys. In Madhya Pradesh, however, it was customary for some votive terracottas to be on wheels, for, whenever a person wanted to express his gratitude to the deity for granting his wishes, he did so by circumambulating the shrine a number of times, dragging his votive terracotta tied to a string behind him. Painted in blue, this object reveals a striking colour scheme.
Coll: Deccan College, Pune.
Photo: Sunil Jadhav.

13. A votive elephant.
Highly conventionalized and decorated with painted stripes, this elephant must have been originally mounted on wheels.
Coll: Deccan College, Pune.
Photo: Sunil Jadhav.

11

12

13

Metal figures.

Tribal metal figures from this region are characterized by the dhokra *technique where the core of the figure is decorated by an overlay of crossed or parallel wires neatly placed close to one another creating a shimmering effect. This tribal technique has inspired modern Indian sculptors.*

14. Elephant howdah with deities.
Probably part of a votive image, it is profusely decorated in the wire technique.
Coll: National Museum, New Delhi.
Photo: courtesy National Museum, New Delhi.

15. Deity riding an elephant.
Coll: National Museum, New Delhi.
Photo: courtesy National Museum, New Delhi.

16. Two equestrian figures.
These images have a remarkable silhouette quality.
Coll: Dr Siddharth and Yashodhara-raje Bhansali.
Photo: Dr Siddharth Bhansali.

17. Two divinities.
Executed in the wire technique these figures stand on an unusual pedestal.
Coll: Dr Siddharth and Yashodhara-raje Bhansali.
Photo: Dr Siddharth Bhansali.

14

16

15

17

Magico-Religious Objects

The tribals of Madhya Pradesh worship many gods and goddesses namely Mahadeo (Shiva), Kali, Devi, Danteswari Devi, Kankalin (Durga), Sat-Bohen, Thakur Dev, Loharjin, Simria, Sitalamata, Ganga Devi, Somiriamata, Biribai, Agwani Devi, Baila Deo, Ghodla Deo, Burimai, Nag, Nandin, Karnakuti, Bangarin, Dulardei, Bhara, Jandu-Bhairam, Mooli, Pardesh, and so on. Representations of some other gods and goddesses on the back of elephants and horses are also found. The proper identification of these gods and goddesses is yet to be ascertained through further research and field investigations.

The forms of the tribal gods and goddesses are basically primitive, though some sophistication has crept in their style and representation in the process of modernization. The Kaser community (also sometimes called Ghadwa) in the villages of the Bastar region made these images of deities for the tribals. They are but a few among the many ritual and ceremonial objects the Kaser community produces. Regardless of whether the image is specially made for the tribals or the non-tribal village peasant it conforms to a traditional design style. Thus, the form remains more or less unchanged and the identification of the deity is based on the attributes it holds. Some of them, doubtless, originated from the Hindu pantheon, but many are of local origin and so it is difficult to say with certainty which of them have strictly tribal affiliations. It is to be noted, however, that Danteswari Devi, identified with the goddess Durga and the tutelary deity of the rulers of the former Bastar state is worshipped by the Gond tribes of Bastar; Kankalin and a few other goddesses are also forms of Durga. By and large, the images which the Kaser community produces for both the tribal and non-tribal groups are not worshipped by individual families but by communities as village ritual figures.

18. Ritual ring.
A symbol of fertility, such rings depicting a farmer with a pair of bullocks, a field with a plentiful harvest, a draw-well, and landlords coming to collect their share are presented to the bride at the time of marriage and are worn for seed-sowing ceremonies.
Coll: National Museum, New Delhi.
Photo: courtesy National Museum, New Delhi.

19. Bastar woman.
Attired in traditional silver ornaments.
Photo : courtesy collection of the late Sumant Moolgaokar — Padma Bhushan.

18

20

20. Muria women.
Stringing flowers for a festive
occasion.
Photo: courtesy and copyright
Jyoti Bhatt.

116

21. Muria dance.
The women dance together forming a chain.
Photo: courtesy Christine Pemberton.

22. Wall decoration.
Painted in black and brown on a white ground with geometrical patterns, this type of decoration occurs commonly among the Rajawar tribes of Madhya Pradesh.
Photo: courtesy and copyright Jyoti Bhatt.

The technique, followed by the Kasers in the manufacture of these images is the same age-old technique of lost wax process. The main raw materials used are usually brass or bell-metal. The pot and the votive lamps which are used in worship are also made of brass or bell-metal. Most of the tribal images are made at Jagdalpur, and the tribes which worship them live in the vicinity of this region.

The last important items of magico-religious purpose used by the tribal people of Madhya Pradesh are the wooden memorial pillars, the anthropomorphic masks, door frames, votive terracottas, and wall-paintings which are considered to be the typical examples of tribal art. The memorial pillars found at Hosangabad, Betul, and Panchmari are masterpieces of tribal wood carving. The pillars are finely carved with human figures in several rows, probably recalling triumphs in war. The anthropomorphic masks representing human faces have been found in the areas in and around Sirpur and Baigachok. These masks are primitive in appearance, and have a close resemblance to those found in the tribal belt of north-eastern India. The door frames used by the Gonds and the Mawasis of Chhindwara are also exquisite examples of carving. The features of the figures appearing on the door frames are either carved in high or low relief and are fairly realistic. In the carving of the human figures, attention is paid to the head which is usually larger in proportion compared to the rest of the body.

The potter's craft is also closely linked with the socio-religious life of the local tribes. The Bastar tribals make the most basic, archetypal terracottas which are simple in form and forceful in expression. Untouched by modern influences their craft has preserved its pristine qualities in conception and execution. This craft is closely associated with the *Pora* festival celebrated in almost all the tribal areas of Madhya Pradesh particularly the Chhattisgarh area. The festivities begin with the ceremonial offerings to the terracotta bull and to their family deity. Goddess Danteswari is offered terracotta elephants; Bhairomdeo (Danteswari's brother-in-law) is offered a horse as a *vahana* (vehicle) and the bull Nandia to Lord Shiva.

The potters also produce all the vessels and images required for the festival. Simultaneously, on the eve of the festival, they may make figures of gods and goddesses and also numerous animals such as the lion, tiger, bull, elephant, horse, and mouse with or without riders. Invariably these are on wheels for the children to play, by dragging and pulling. It may be noted here that though the tribals themselves fashion the unbaked clay figures, they do not make terracottas. Nevertheless it is clear that in terracotta, both the potter's craft and creativity, and the tribal's soul play a very important part.

The tribals also offer votive terracotta figures of animals at large sanctuaries in special places away from their villages to fulfil specific vows. When a tribal cannot go to a large sanctuary, he places his offerings at the miniature sanctuary in his own village.

The tribals of Madhya Pradesh are also fond of painting the walls of their thatched huts. To their untutored minds there is in line and form not only the power of aesthetics but the vibrance of the actuality symbolized. Their paintings made in joy and happiness, harmony and worship are votive statements that plead for continued benevolence and protection from the "Evil Eye". The tribals believe that through their paintings the spirits are satisfied. The gods in their grandeur, the forest trees and fields, the huts, and the implements that together form the sum total of their environment become the subject of their paintings.

The tribals generally paint the walls of their homes during the harvest season or at weddings, births, and other festive occasions. Fertility for man and field, health and vigour—this is what the paintings supplicate for. To the tribal people art is not a mere form of expression but is a wild surge of creativity that breaks the banks of life's stilting monotony in a flood of fantasy.

The study of the tribal crafts of Madhya Pradesh reveals the innate artistic taste of the tribal people and their desire to combine utility with beauty. The tribal art of this central state firstly, shows a tendency towards abstraction; secondly, it is more or less an applied art specially in its origin; and thirdly, though it is conservative, it is akin to the universal art of the simple and the sophisticated people of the world.

N. DEVASAHAYAM AND GEETA SALI

SOUTH INDIA

In south India, the region comprising Karnataka, Andhra Pradesh, Tamil Nadu, and Kerala, there are more than a hundred tribal communities. Prominent among them are the Chenchus and Lambadis of Andhra Pradesh, and the Todas and Badagas of Tamil Nadu. Originally, these tribes were hill or forest dwellers, but now there is an increasing tendency to come down to the plains. However, in spite of being near the villages and towns, they tend to segregate themselves and live as secluded groups.

The tribals of southern India are quite simple in their way of life. Their main possessions are a few utensils made of earthenware or cheap metals, bamboo containers, gourd shells, baskets, some clothes, as well as hunting and fishing equipment. Their artistic expression is primary and is confined chiefly to personal adornment–dress, textiles, and decorative accessories such as combs, and some utilitarian objects.

The Chenchus, interestingly enough, find mention in the *Manusmriti,* an indication of their early existence in Andhra Pradesh. Even today they are found chiefly in this region, in the rugged hills with steep slopes and deep forested valleys.

The word "Chenchu" means a person living under the *chettu* tree. A legend among the Chenchus claims that the female deity Bhramaramba of Shrishailam hails from their tribe and that Lord Mallikarjuna fell in love with her. Another legend also connects this tribe with Lord Mallikarjuna of Shrishailam. According to this legend, there was a girl who lived alone under the *chettu* tree subsisting on wild fruits and berries. Because she lived under the *chettu* tree she was known as Chenchita. One day Lord Mallikarjuna chanced to see her and fell in love with her. He married her and their descendants are the Chenchus.

There are various theories that trace the descent of the Todas to the Scythians, remnants of Alexander's invading army, the Pandavas of the Indian epic lore, the Pallava dynastic rulers, or the Sumerians. There is no convincing evidence to connect them to any of these groups. They seem to belong to the southern region with linguistic affinities to the Tamil language, parallels in social and cultural customs to those prevalent in Malabar, and religious affiliation to the Hindu temple of Nanjankundi at Mysore.

The Todas live in the scenic surroundings of the Nilgiri Hills in Tamil Nadu. They are a pastoral people and subsist on the products of their buffaloes. The men spend their time in herding, milking their buffaloes, and churning milk, while the women look after the household chores. The Todas do not till the land and depend on the supply of grains from the Badagas, a neighbouring tribe that is predominantly agricultural. The Kotas, another tribe in that region, who specialize primarily in crafts supply the Todas with pottery and ironware. They also provide music in Toda ceremonials because the Todas do not play music – it is tabooed in their tribe.

The Lambadis, a wandering tribe, also known by the name of Banjara and Lamane are of mixed origin. They are mentioned in the work of Dandi, *Dashakumara Charita.* There are a couple of legends about their origin. According to one, they trace their origin to Mola, a cowherd of Lord Krishna. Yet, according to another legend, they are the descendants of the famous monkey kings Vali and Sugriva of the *Ramayana.* According to the first legend Mola and his wife were childless; they approached a king and exhibited the art of gymnastics in which Mola was adept. The king was so pleased with his art that he gave him three children for adoption. In time they grew up and their progeny gave rise to different groups of Lambadis. As regards the name of the tribe, Banjara or Lambadi, it seems to have been derived from the fact that they are wanderers dealing in grains and salt. Different theories put the derivation of the name to different words, such as the Persian "Beriaj Arind" meaning rice dealer, the Sanskrit word "Banij" signifying merchant, "Lavan" meaning salt or "Lamban" meaning length, the last word probably referring to the long line in which they move their caravans. The Lambadis play a very important role during wartime by supplying the forces with food and also spying. Being a nomadic tribe, they do not have permanent dwellings.

Dwellings

With the exception of the Chenchus and the Todas, most of the tribes in this region erect temporary and flimsy huts. The Chenchus decorate their simple wattle hut doors with a design consisting of broad, alternate green and white bands. The Toda huts called *ars* on the other hand, are well designed, being reminiscent of early rock-hewn cave temples in plan and elevation. Made of thatch and bamboo with wooden beams, they are half barrel-vaulted and circular or rectangular in plan. One to six residential areas with their buffalo-pen and the

1. Terracotta bowl with lid.
Although the art of making clay figurines seems to have died out completely in the southern region, its existence in earlier centuries is known from human and animal figures recovered from Nilgiri burial sites.
Coll: Madras Museum.
Photo: courtesy and copyright V.K. Rajamani.

The Todas.

The Todas live in scenic surroundings in the Nilgiri Hills of Tamil Nadu. A pastoral people, they subsist on the products of their buffaloes and barter them for grain and other requirements.

sacred dairy, constitute a Toda *mund* or village. The dairy is the temple of the Todas and the dairymen their priests! In structure the dairy is similar to the residential hut. Women are forbidden entrance to the sacred dairy.

Textiles

In their dress, the Todas and the Lambadis reveal a highly developed aesthetic sense. The Toda *putkuli* (shawl) is striking in its bold colour scheme and its complex combination of weaving and embroidery. Made of coarse white homespun cloth, approximately 76.3 x 259.3 cm., it consists of two lengths (each length consisting of two pieces joined longitudinally) of cloth sewn together at the edges to form a garment of double thickness. The design is laid out in strips of crimson and black which are woven in the cloth at the two ends−one end being more elaborate than the other. On these strips and between them, embroidery is carried out in intricate designs by means of darning and by counting the threads of the woven material to give shape to the motif. When the embroidery is done along the strip, and not across it, geometrical patterns appear on the reverse of the shawl as well. The popular embroidery motifs are: butterfly, eyes of the peacock's tail feather, zigzags, squares, and loops. The squirrel and the snake motifs are also commonly employed. Generally, a *putkuli* with the snake motif is used as a shroud. The *putkuli* is worn among the Todas by both the men and the women. The best and most elaborately worked specimens are used by important persons of the tribe, at festive gatherings, and funerals. The elderly people store the more intricately designed shawls to be draped over their bodies when they are dead.

The clothes of the Lambadi women reveal bright colours in bold contrasts. They are embroidered, studded with mirrors and glass, and edged with cowrie shells. The embroidery is carried out in geometric patterns in beautifully blended colours. The rank of the woman is shown by the way she wears a stick on the head. In fact, the stick rests on the head like a huge comb on which the shoulder robe is drawn. The Lambadi women wear a considerable amount of jewellery including long ear-rings attached to the hair. They also use a number of hairpins. Their appearance is extremely colourful and immediately striking.

Ornaments

The Toda women who are noted for wearing their hair in ringlets adorn themselves with ornaments such as necklaces, ear-rings, armlets, bangles, and anklets. They also wear a distinctive ornament called the *tulwaji,* a crude and heavy brass ring weighing almost two

2. Toda hut.
Toda huts, known as *ars*, are well designed and constructed. In plan and elevation they are reminiscent of cave temples with barrel vaults and circular or rectangular floor areas. The Toda women curl their hair in ringlets, have tattooed body decorations, and wear the *putkuli* − a shawl with red and black patterns.
Photo: courtesy Christine Pemberton.

Textiles and Ornaments.

The textiles of the Todas and Lambadis reveal a highly developed aesthetic sense. Their ornaments conform to the usual types found among other Indian tribal communities.

3. *Putkuli.*
Made of white homespun cloth, it consists of two pieces of material stitched back to back and embroidered in red and black. The two ends are elaborately decorated. These patterns are executed by the combined methods of darning and embroidery. Because the design is executed by counting threads it results in angular forms.
Coll: Sankho Choudhuri.
Photo: Datta Gupta.

kilograms which is worn on the upper arm. They wear massive anklets of carved bison-horn, bracelets made of fibre, and tassels with cowrie shells arranged in a wide petalled flower pattern. The Toda men also wear ear-rings.

The Lambadi women are very fond of ornaments. The characteristic ornaments of the Lambadi women are the ivory bangles worn along the length of the arm, from the shoulder to the wrist. Sometimes they are dyed red. In some parts, the women wear pieces of copper round their neck, fresh each time during a pregnancy, to propitiate the tribal goddess. Brass or horn anklets with jingling bells are also worn. *Cheed,* a string of beads of ten or twenty rows with a cowrie as a pendant is also a favourite ornament of this tribe. Anklets of ivory or bone or horn are worn by married women.

Women from the Paniyan tribe wear an ear stud called *olai* made from the solidified milk of the jack fruit tree. A large stud cut from this and embedded with red seeds is put in dilated holes in the ear lobes—stretching them almost to splitting point. The women from the Kadar tribe wear scrolls of plaited *ithai,* a kind of reed similar to the bamboo, in their ear lobes.

4

4. Banjara embroidery.
In contrast with the sober and limited palette of the Toda *putkuli,* the Banjara embroideries are lively and colourful. The forms, here, also are geometric and executed by skilful blending of colours. The tribal character is emphasized by the cowrie shells used as edging to the piece.
Coll: Chester and Davida Herwitz Family Collection.
Photo: courtesy Chester and Davida Herwitz.

The Kota tribals are expert at making ornaments in different types of metals such as iron and gold. They make bangles, ear-rings, and a variety of necklaces to supply to other tribals in the area.

Many Indian tribes consider a hair comb important not only as a decorative ornament but also as an item with symbolic meaning. In several tribes, it has romantic associations because it is presented by the man to the girl he loves. In other tribes the bridegroom presents it to his bride during the marriage ceremony, and at such times the comb has ritual significance.

Among the Chenchus the comb is devoid of any special connotation. The men carve the comb handles with exquisite designs consisting of zigzag bands and triangles in low relief. The Kadar bride receives a five-pronged comb made of bamboo from the bridegroom at the time of marriage. It is prepared specially by the groom and is ceremonial in nature. It is embellished with geometric symbols, the rhythmic and symmetrical repetitions of which reveal a highly developed sensibility. The comb is shaped like a "V" and is worn in the front. It is a token of love, and a seal and sign of marriage. In the Muduvar tribe, it is customary for a young man

5

5. Bangles.
These bangles belong to the Kota tribe in the Kotagiri region of the Nilgiris. The Kotas are primarily an artisan community that supply other neighbouring tribals with pottery and ironware.
Coll: Madras Museum.
Photo: courtesy and copyright V.K. Rajamani.

6. Ornaments.
Photo: courtesy Sankho Choudhuri.

6

125

to present a comb to the girl he wishes to marry. The comb, made of bamboo, has a decorative etched design on it and has a pointed knob on top. The comb is the symbol of marriage and a Muduvar woman will wear it always. She wears it at the back of her head. The difference between the Kadar and Muduvar combs lies in their shapes and the style of wearing them.

Tattoo

The women in the Toda, the Lambadi, and the Chenchu tribes of south India show a predilection for tattooed decorations. The designs are geometrical or naturalistic and are executed on the arms, chest, and legs. The Todas have specific designs—semicircles of dots on the outside of each arm, a double row of dots on the chest, a solitary dot on the chin, and two circular lines of dots on each leg. The Lambadi women prefer elaborate designs on the backs of their hands and a dot on the left side of the nose.

Baskets

The tribal people have become very adept in the art of making baskets and mats from bamboo and the *ithai*. In the southern regions the Chenchus and the Kadars are proficient in the technique of wicker work. They use different methods for different parts of the basket to obtain the desired result. For example, the body of the basket generally consists of broad twisted strips, a twined rim, and a base constructed in lattice pattern.

Baskets are made in different sizes and shapes to suit their purpose. Round, shallow, pan-types are suited for drying fruits while a basket with a broad mouth and narrow base is for collecting fruits and *mahua* flowers. A small basket with a lid serves as a receptacle for ornaments. Large baskets are plastered with clay mixed with cowdung and grass for storing grains. The Chenchus specialize in the making of baskets for honey which are globular and made of fine bamboo strips. The basket is smeared with resin to make it leak-proof.

A bamboo jug is used by Todas to store milk. It is decorated tastefully. According to a legend, these bamboo jugs known as *phenn* serve as symbolic representations of the golden milk vessels which were permanently left in the other world.

Pottery

Only the Kotas of Nilgiri and the Urali Kurumbas of Kerala practise the art of pottery. The Kota women make pots on a small turntable operated by hand, while the Urali Kurumbas make a pot by first shaping it by hand, then beating it with a light wooden beater until it assumes the required shape, and then scooping out the clay from inside the pot. The pot is then decorated with an incised design. The Urali Kurumba is the only tribe in India that uses the scooped-out method.

Musical Instruments

The Kotas, the Chenchus, and the Urali Kurumbas make a limited number of musical instruments such as drums and flutes. The Chenchus use a wind instrument made of two river reeds and a gourd. It is capable of producing remarkable variations in tune. Occasionally, this instrument has incised decorations and one superb example depicts a tiger chasing a stag. This is probably an expression that is not standardized in style and content.

The tribes of southern India, simple as they are in their way of life, still continue with primitive art-forms and decorative practices found only on household objects such as vessels, baskets or on clothing. The artistic design tends, largely, to be pristine in nature, confined to etchings and that too usually elementary and geometrical in form. Occasionally, the forms show surprising complexity in their concept, as well their execution, as in the Toda textiles, or the Chenchu musical instruments, though neither is as profuse in production nor as artistic in expression as the artefacts of some other tribes. In India, the art-forms of southern India conform to the traditions and sensibilities that characterize tribal India. The Muduvar combs, the Chenchu baskets, the Toda textiles as well as the Kota pottery are essentially, regional manifestations of a much wider cultural spectrum.

SUJIT SOM

BAY
ISLANDS

The idea of art lies in the manifestation of the imaginative expressions of the human mind. Such an expression in any population group is generally found in different working media such as paintings, sculpture, basketry, weaving, body decoration, and clothing. Again, art is also an embodiment of creative processes which manipulate movements, sounds, words or materials. Certain art-forms arose out of utilitarian considerations and there can be little doubt that certain essential requirements paved the way for creativity. Thus, the contextual setting in which art is produced and used differs not only from person to person but also from one group to another.

The history of the Andaman and Nicobar Islands has passed through different phases of cross-cultural interactions. The aborigines – altogether six distinct population groups – live in certain pockets. In the Bay of Bengal a broken chain of five hundred and fifty-six islands located between the Cape Negrais of Myanmar in the north and the Achin Head of Sumatra in Indonesia in the south, is the union territory of Andaman and Nicobar Islands known as the Bay Islands. The archipelago is seven hundred kilometres in length. These islands are divided into two groups: the Andaman group and the Nicobar group. In the former there are twenty-six islands that have human habitation while in the latter there are twelve. These two groups are separated by a one hundred and forty-four kilometre wide channel which also serves as an ethnological, ecological, technological, and cultural barrier.

The existence of the Negritos of the Andamans – the Great Andamanese, the Onge, the Jarawa, and the Sentinelese, as well as the Mongoloids of the Nicobar – the Nicobarese and the Shompen can be traced back to a distant past. There are several theories as to how these tribes came to these isolated islands but none of them can be generally authenticated for want of satisfactory records. However, it is generally accepted that four aboriginal tribes of the Andaman Islands belong to the Negrito group and portray cultural affinities to the South-East Asiatic Negritos of the Malaya Peninsula and the Aeta of the Philippines. This would indicate that they must have migrated to the Andaman Islands from South-East Asia either by sea or by land many centuries ago. But now these tribes face a threat of degeneration as revealed from various census reports.

The origins of the Nicobarese are obscure but it appears that their population is increasing. However, among them, the Mongoloid group – the Shompen – is gradually declining. The Negritos of the Andamans are food gatherers and hunters whereas the Mongoloids of Nicobar

Bay Islands

In the Bay of Bengal a broken chain of five hundred and forty-six islands form the Indian Union Territory of the Andaman and Nicobar Islands. Known as the Bay Islands, they form two groups of islands—the Andaman and the Nicobar.

2

1. A mythical bird.
Placed outside the hut, this magico-religious bird is installed to protect the inhabitants from evil spirits.
Nicobar Islands.
Photo: courtesy and copyright Jyoti Bhatt.

2. Body decorations of smeared clay.
The Onge tribe practise a form of decoration whereby a thick paste obtained from a mixture of clay and water is applied in bold curving strokes emphasizing the contours of the body.
Andaman Islands.
Photo: courtesy and copyright M.K. Pal.

3. *El-panam.*
The tribal hut is shaped like a beehive and is called *el-panam.*
Nicobar Islands.
Photo: courtesy and copyright Jyoti Bhatt.

4

are gardeners. Only the Shompen among the tribals of Nicobar are between the Negritos and the Nicobarese: they practise gathering and hunting as well as gardening. The tribes practise inter-island trade by way of barter.

Among the Negritos of the Andamans, art is reflected in the objects of material culture such as scooped out wooden buckets and intricately designed cane baskets. Artistic skills and traditional techniques are revealed in the shaping of a tree (Sterculia species) in the form of a sea-going canoe and the tassel made of yellow dried skin of Dendrodium plants as observed in the women's dress. Religion among the Negritos is in incipient form, though they subscribe to a system which believes in the survival of the spirit after death and fear its return.

Tattooing is not found among the Onges of the Andamans. But body decorations are made with a paste of plain grey clay, mixed with water, in the form of coarse patterns while delicate and fine patterns are executed in white clay. Red ochre mixed with turtle, pig, or almond oil is smeared over the body with patterns. The general practice is for the wife to decorate the body of her husband, but she smears her body by herself.

Again, a system of body decoration or tattooing is prevalent among both sexes of the Great Andamanese tribes. They do this by cutting their bodies with small flakes of quartz or glass in patterns of zigzags or straight lines running up and down the body. Each cut, about a quarter of an inch in length, is superficial. To make a pattern of straight lines, an incision is made and about one eighth of an inch is then cut. Twelve to fourteen such lines will make the required patterns of their choice. In the zigzag pattern only two lines are made, the cuts being incised at obtuse angles to each other, and thus forming a dog-tooth pattern which the women execute. The first cutting is made from the navel to the pubis. The face, ears, arms, and knee-pits are never cut. The dog-tooth patterns are often cut on either side of an imaginary line running from the sternum to the navel, imitating, as it were, the edges of an open waistcoat.

Different types of body decoration are prevalent among the neighbouring groups. The cuts are made by a man, with the head of a pig arrow and are severe and deep. They are made across the body or limb, and are not placed end to end but parallel to each other. They are about an inch in length and half an inch apart. As a rule, three lines of cuts are made: one in the centre of the back from the nape of the neck to the buttocks, and one on either side of

4. Standing scare-devil.
A bold life-sized gesticulating figure, attired in straw, stands in a bamboo hut to chase devils away.
Nicobar Islands.
Photo: courtesy and copyright Jyoti Bhatt.

5. Scare-devil.
The unpredictable climate, the unyielding land, the rough seas, and isolation have led to great hardship for the people living in the Bay Islands. The Nicobarese believe that evil spirits cause suffering and pain and must be appeased constantly through votive offerings or be frightened away by magical means.
Courtesy Rashtriya Manav Sangrahalaya, Bhopal.
Photo: courtesy and copyright Jyoti Bhatt.

5

6. *Henta-koi.*
Characterized by forcefulness and power, such wooden figures are kept in the homes of the Bay Islanders at the time of sickness, to scare away the demon causing the disease. If the patient recovers, the figure is kept in the house but if he or she dies, it is thrown into the sea.
Coll: National Museum, New Delhi.
Photo: courtesy National Museum, New Delhi.

7. Interior of an *el-panam.*
Mainly made of wood the hut houses ancestor effigies which are worshipped.
Courtesy Rashtriya Manav Sangrahalaya, Bhopal.
Photo: courtesy and copyright Jyoti Bhatt.

8. Three seated ancestral figures.
Placed inside the house, these figures are regularly offered a feast consisting of food, intoxicating spirits, and a *bidi.*
Photo: courtesy and copyright Jyoti Bhatt.

9. Ancestral figure.
The figure bedecked with jewellery and clothing sits calmly in a chair.
Nicobar Islands.
Courtesy Rashtriya Manav Sangrahalaya, Bhopal.
Photo: courtesy and copyright Jyoti Bhatt.

10. A seated female figure.
The vermilion spot on the forehead and beaded ornaments indicate that this figure is a woman.
Photo: courtesy and copyright Jyoti Bhatt.

this central line – from each shoulder to halfway down to the buttocks. These lines are about three inches apart. Occasionally four or five lines of smaller cuts, about two inches apart, are also made from the collar-bone to the pubis. Other smaller lines of cuts are also made, sometimes encircling the arms and legs, the sloping cuts resemble the slats of a half-open venetian blind. The women of this group, as a rule, get sear marked when they become elderly. The two remaining Negrito tribes of the Andamans – the Jarawas and the Sentinelese – have not been discussed here as there is no authenticated information about them.

The aboriginal inhabitants of the Nicobar Islands are the Nicobarese while the interior parts of the Great Nicobar Island are occupied by the Nicobarese or the Holchu. Among the Nicobarese, the *hori* (the canoe) and the earthern pot made by the Chowrans represent two important artistic traditions. The skill in manufacturing an all-season seagoing canoe is known only to the inhabitants of the central and southern group of islanders. Their canoes are highly prized among the islanders. Canoes manufactured by the Pulo Milo and Kondul tribes exhibit excellent craftsmanship. Canoes made for racing are decorated on the sides with beautiful patterns in many colours. The Chowran pot is made by the coiling technique. The clay required for the pot is collected by the men while the women are responsible for making the pots without the aid of a wheel. The women undertake the work only after making a ritual offering of a pig or a chicken and the blood is sprinkled on the potter's body to ward off *Iwi* or evil spirits and to ensure the successful completion of the process. The climate and the geographical situation compel the Nicobarese to engage themselves in their economic activities throughout the year. The barter system and inter-island trade relationships permit the arts and crafts to continue uninterruptedly.

The unpredictable climate, the unyielding land, the rough surrounding sea, natural disasters, and restricted communication facilities, cause grave hardship and suffering among the islanders. All these calamities, the Nicobarese believe, are due to evil spirits, and also the spirit of the dead *me-ala-ha*. The islanders credit these spirits with powers that can bring sickness, damage to property, and harm to individuals. They believe that this evil spirit must be continuously appeased and propitiated by offerings or be frightened away by magical means. Such offerings of spirit scarers, *kareau,* are most common in all the traditional dwellings, known as *el-panam*. The *kareau* take the form of carved human figures of various sizes, representations of mythical animals, fish, crocodiles, or birds. They are kept in prominent places in the house. The devil, in the form of a special spirit scarer, is mostly found outside the house. *Iwi-ka,* the benevolent spirits, are honoured by arranging occasional family spirit feasts while the malevolent spirits in different forms of *kareau* are appeased through sacrifices and thus kept at bay.

The Nicobarese in general are superstitious and strong believers in *Iwi. Menluana,* the witch doctor, plays a significant role as a medium communicating with spirits and in making scare-devils of different forms. Simultaneously, to control the spirits of surrounding sea animals, effigies of the animals are made of wood and are appeased by the performance of sympathetic magic.

The concept of art-form among the Nicobarese is centred around the sculptured figures of the scare-devils. In form and style these figures differ considerably from one group to another. Some of the artistic expressions noticeable in carved wooden figures, with squarish modelling representing ancestral spirits, undoubtedly reveal a developed style.

Henta paintings are found in most of the Nicobarese villages. These, not only express the extent of artistic skill but are also integral to the magico-religious beliefs and practices of the tribes. In all such cases lively expression dominates artistic form. The scare-devils are of two broad varieties – *henta* and *henta koi,* found mostly in the central group of the islands.

Henta paintings are worked on areca spathe screens or carved on boards with considerable simplicity. Some screens contain even seven or eight pictures but ordinarily four are painted on one screen. A representation of the sun surmounts the whole design, or the sun and the moon are represented at the top right and left corners. A man, probably representing an anthropomorphic conception of god known as "Deuse", is portrayed in a standing posture and dressed in some quaint garb. On the other side of the screen various weapons, implements, and articles of daily use are depicted. Below the figure of the "Deuse", huts, coconut trees, pigs, birds, and sometimes men as well as women are shown. Animals, canoes, fish, mermaids, and crocodiles are depicted at the bottom of the paintings.

A *henta* from Camorta Island locally known as *runi* is a dome-shaped board used for

11. A priest with his ancestor's skull.
Nicobar Islands.
Photo: courtesy and copyright Jyoti Bhatt.

12. Priest with ancestor figure.
An old Nicobarese priest with his assistant sits inside an *el-panam* next to an ancestor effigy and a dog carved in wood. According to a prevailing legend, "a pregnant young woman was forced to leave her native country (Burma) and come to Nicobar with a dog. All Nicobarese are her descendants." Nicobar Islands.
Photo: courtesy and copyright Jyoti Bhatt.

appeasing the evil spirit responsible for the problems at the time of menstruation of women. The painting is composed in three strata. At the central point of the board a figure of a girl in traditional attire is partly carved and partly painted. The face is emphasized by carving it in relief. The bottom stratum portrays sea life, while the centre one depicts life on land with some scenes including a traditional Nicobarese *el-panam,* coconut trees, women at work, pigs, and canoes. The upper stratum reveals motifs such as the sun, moon, stars, and flowers. Paintings of this type hold a socio-religious significance and serve as protection as well.

Similarly, the *henta-koi,* consists mostly of figures carved in wood. Some of the figures are real, some imaginative or mythical. In addition to human figures, real or mythical figures of animals, birds, fish, crocodiles, and ladders, carved or painted in various colours show an aggressive and monstrous character. The intention is to scare away the devil or spirit. Such figures are generally used at the time of sickness in the house. If the patient recovers, then these figures are preserved, otherwise they are thrown into the sea and are replaced with new ones. The motif of the ladder is particularly important as it is used for discovering the evil spirit in the air while the ship or the canoe is supposed to enable the tribals to find the spirit in the coastal villages. The representations of fish, birds, and animals are meant to invoke their assistance and goodwill in discovering these offending spirits.

A *henta-koi* carving of a bird is for propitiating the spirit known as *henta-koi-kalang.* A single representation of "Deuse" on a board or an areca spathe is termed as *henta-to-oninya.* Similarly, *henyan-gashi-heng* represents the sun with a human face and eight arms among which his children are shown, *henyan-gashi-kahe* signifies the moon.

The practice of this type of art-form — effigies and paintings — in far-flung isolated islands is based exclusively on magico-religious concepts directed towards the fulfilment of certain beliefs within the accepted social norms. In such art-forms, neither the role of the artist nor the aesthetic quality is important.

Thus, the tribal art-forms of the Bay Islands reveal two distinct trends: one slightly rudimentary form evident in the material cultural objects of the Negritos of the Andamans and the other, the mixed forms arising from the magico-religious beliefs and practices of the Nicobarese people.